THE WEIMAR REPUBLIC

The Weimar Republic
SECOND EDITION

J W HIDEN

LONGMAN
LONDON AND NEW YORK

Addison Wesley Longman Limited,
Edinburgh Gate,
Harlow, Essex CM20 2JE, United Kingdom
and Associated Companies throughout the world.

*Published in the United States of America
by Addison Wesley Longman, New York*

© Longman Group Limited 1974
© Addison Wesley Longman Limited 1996

First published 1974
Nineteenth impression 1994
Second edition 1996

ISBN 0 582 28706 5 PPR

British Library Cataloguing-in-Publication Data

A catalogue record for this book is
available from the British Library

Library of Congress Cataloging-in-Publication Data

Set by 7 in 10/12 Sabon Roman
Produced through Longman Malaysia, PP

CONTENTS

Editorial Foreword		vii
Note on referencing system		viii
Acknowledgements		ix
Abbreviations		x
	PART ONE: BACKGROUND	**1**
1.	CONSTITUTION: AFTER REVOLUTION	1
2.	VERSAILLES: TRUTH AND FICTION	9
	PART TWO: PROBLEMS	**15**
3.	COALITIONS AND PARTY POLITICS	15
4.	FOREIGN POLICY	22
5.	ECONOMICS AND REPARATIONS	30
6.	LEFTIST OPPOSITION	36
7.	RIGHTIST OPPOSITION	42
8.	*REICHSWEHR* AND POLITICS	50
	PART THREE: CONCLUSION	**58**
9.	THE CRISIS AND HITLER	58
	PART FOUR: DOCUMENTS	**72**
	Bibliography	101
	Index	114

For Hugo

EDITORIAL FOREWORD

Such is the pace of historical enquiry in the modern world that there is an ever-widening gap between the specialist article or monograph, incorporating the results of current research, and general surveys, which inevitably become out of date. *Seminar Studies in History* are designed to bridge this gap. The books are written by experts in their field who are not only familiar with the latest research but have often contributed to it. They are frequently revised, in order to take account of new information and interpretations. They provide a selection of documents to illustrate major themes and provoke discussion, and also a guide to further reading. Their aim is to clarify complex issues without over-simplifying them, and to stimulate readers into deepening their knowledge and understanding of major themes and topics.

ROGER LOCKYER
General Editor

NOTE ON REFERENCING SYSTEM

Readers should note that numbers in square brackets [5] refer them to the corresponding entry in the Bibliography at the end of the book (specific page numbers are given in italics). A number in square brackets preceded by *Doc.* [*Doc. 5*] refers readers to the corresponding item in the Documents section which follows the main text.

ACKNOWLEDGEMENTS

The publishers would like to thank the following for permission to reproduce copyright material:

Harald Boldt Verlag GmbH for an extract from *Das Kabinet Muller II Akten der Reichskanzlei Weimarer Republik*, Vol. 2 pp. 1246–7, edited by Marin Vogt; an extract from *The Germans and Their Modern History*, by Franz Ernst. Copyright © 1966 by Columbia University Press. Reprinted with permission of the publisher; an extract reprinted from *Political Institutions of the German Revolution, 1918–1919*, edited by C.B. Burdick and R.H. Lutz, with the publisher, Hoover Institution Press. Copyright © 1966 by the Board of Trustees of the Leland Stanford Junior University; Karl Rauch Verlag, Dusseldorf 1968 for extracts from *Der Aufstieg der NSDAP in Augenzeugenberichten*, 3rd edition, pp. 306–7 and 347–8, edited by E. Deuerlein; extracts from *The Reichswehr and Politics 1918–1933*, by F.L. Carsten, pp. 12, 94–5 and 140–1, published in 1966, *The German Inflation of 1923*, by F.K. Ringer, pp. 112–13 published in 1969, an extract taken from *Hitler's Speeches*, Vol. 1, by N.H. Baynes, pp. 13–14, published in 1942 by permission of Oxford University Press; an extract from *Documents on Nazism 1919–1945* edited by J. Noakes and G. Pridham, page 128 published in 1974 reprinted by permission of the Peters Fraser & Dunlop Group Ltd; an extract from *Through Two Decades* by Theodor Wolff, pp. 138–9 published by William Heinemann reprinted by permission of Reed Consumer Books Ltd.

Whilst every effort has been made to trace the owners of copyright material, the publishers take this opportunity to offer our apologies to any copyright holders whose rights we may have unwittingly infringed.

ABBREVIATIONS

BVP   Bavarian People's Party (*Bayerische Volkspartei*)

DDP   German Democratic Party (*Deutsche Demokratische Partei*)

DVP   German People's Party (*Deutsche Volkspartei*)

DNVP   German National People's Party – Nationalists (*Deutschnationale Volkspartei*)

KAPD   German Communist Workers' Party (*Kommunistische Arbeiter Partei Deutschlands*)

KPD   German Communist Party (*Kommunistische Partei Deutschlands*)

NSDAP   National Socialist German Workers' Party (*Nationalsozialistische Deutsche Arbeiterpartei*)

SA   Storm Detachment (*Sturmabteilung*)

SPD   German Social Democratic Party (*Sozialdemokratische Partei Deutschlands*)

SS   Protection Squads (*Schutzstaffeln*)

USPD   German Independent Social Democratic Party (*Unabhängige Sozialdemokratische Partei Deutschlands*)

PART ONE: BACKGROUND

1 CONSTITUTION: AFTER REVOLUTION

In the light of our knowledge of the tragic end of the Weimar Republic it appears difficult to quarrel with Golo Mann's admonition on the subject of the Weimar constitution: 'What is put down on paper at the beginning will influence future events without determining them' [29 p. 572]. The more optimistic view expressed by an English historian writing in 1926 reminds us, however, at least to make the effort to understand how things looked before anyone had imagined the seizure of power by the National Socialists. 'German democracy', wrote Gooch, 'which was born in the trenches and inspired the revolution, found permanent expression in the Weimar constitution' [22]. Whilst both authors, writing forty years apart, regarded the constitution as a framework which had to bear the weight of future developments, Gooch more aptly stressed that the constitution was also the product of the past and that this process partly determined what was 'put down on paper'. The point can be illustrated by briefly examining the transition from the German Empire to the Weimar Republic during the German revolution of 1918–19.

Although democratisation was taking place slowly in Germany before and during the First World War, the wave of revolutionary disturbances which swept the country after the German Fleet's refusal to put to sea at Kiel on 28 October 1918 owed at least as much to war weariness as it did to political pressures [43; 56]. The revulsion against war was intensified by the sudden shock of Germany's imminent defeat after four years of fighting. Through ignorance, impatience or scepticism, the German masses paid little attention to the ill-publicised constitutional reforms of October 1918. These went hand in hand with the effective loss of power by the 'military dictatorship' of the wartime leaders, Generals Ludendorff and Hindenburg [48]. In spite of the fact that the reforms turned the Empire into a constitutional monarchy, most Germans continued to regard the Kaiser as the reason for past troubles, the cause of their present suffering and the most important remaining obstacle to the signature of an armistice to end hostilities with the Allied Powers. In the face of such pressure, existing order virtually collapsed. The rapid spread throughout Germany of workers' and soldiers' councils confirmed that people were also attracted by the prospect of far-reaching political change [55]. The Kaiser abdicated and power logically went to the party of the masses. In the first place then, the revolution was one which brought the German socialists to power. The Republic was proclaimed on 9 November 1918 and an all-socialist government was set up on the following day. But what sort of socialists were now in control?

Although the time seemed ripe for a remodelling of society and a clean break with the imperial past, German socialists were neither fully prepared for revolution nor united. The majority of the Social Democratic Party (*Sozialdemokratische Partei Deutschlands* – SPD), led by Friedrich Ebert, found it difficult to escape from pre-war categories of thinking and strategy. German socialists had tended, in practice, to play down their revolutionary programme, drawn up in Erfurt in 1891, and had settled down to work for reforms, including a genuine constitutional monarchy [120; 122]. Their programme was partly implemented in October and its completion seemed likely with the Republic's proclamation. It was thus Ebert's intention to restore the conditions necessary to the holding of elections to a National Assembly [41; 47; 51]. The larger body would then have the responsibility of drawing up the proposed new constitution. Naturally, the SPD leadership anticipated that with the collapse of the old state the elections would return the sort of socialist majorities who would restructure German society soon enough.

Other socialists were less sanguine. A minority had broken away from the parent body as early as April 1917 to form the Independent German Social Democratic Party (*Unabhängige Sozial-demokratische Partei Deutschlands* – USPD). The split was occasioned less by ideological differences, although these existed, and more by personality clashes and arguments over tactics, in particular regarding how socialists should respond to the First World War. Most of the USPD leaders did not envisage the revolution in Germany following the pattern of the upheaval which had brought the Bolsheviks to power in Russia in October 1917. On the other hand, USPD leaders such as Hugo Haase were shrewd enough to demand a more positive and immediate approach to the restructuring of German society and its economy. They felt that opportunities had to be grasped and a new order consolidated before the elections to the National Assembly, forestalling if possible a regrouping of the powerful conservative forces and a check to further reform [*Docs 1, 3*]. Haase and others therefore deplored the hesitant and cautious stance of Ebert and his supporters [168].

It was, of course, hoped that the problems of revolution would reunite German socialists in a common purpose – a wish finding expression in the composition of the Provisional Government formed on 10 November 1918. This Council of Peoples' Commissars, with its three SPD and three USPD members, derived its fundamental authority from the workers' and soldiers' councils. There remained the pressing problem of the third group of socialists known as the Spartacists, who had formed themselves on an anti-war basis round Karl Liebknecht in 1914 and included in their ranks such charismatic leaders as Rosa Luxemburg and Franz Mehring. Although still attached to the USPD until they formed the German Communist Party (*Kommunistische Partei Deutschlands* – KPD) in December 1918, the Spartacists *did* propagate the seizure of power on the Russian model once revolution broke out in Germany. Together with an important grouping of radical shop stewards, the Spartacists were a formidable pressure group for the new government to contend with [160]. Although not endorsing the Spartacist programme, the USPD leaders were extremely sensitive to the pull of the far left. Moreover, they soon found themselves exasperated by Ebert's own zealous response to the exaggerated threat of communism. Such internal tensions combined to frustrate hopes for socialist unity, thwarting those who longed to hammer out a new socio-economic order.

The SPD leadership remained committed to suppressing threats from extremists, which was wholly consistent with Ebert's own conception of the revolution as the moderate democratisation of the German state [47]. Nevertheless, Ebert was severely criticised for working closely with the discredited officer corps of Wilhelmine Germany during the revolution and for generally underestimating the threat from the right. The support of the armed forces, conveyed by General Wilhelm Groener to Ebert on 10 November 1918 (see Chapter 8) and duly accepted by the latter, further inflamed the overall political situation [42]. It deepened the existing unease in the USPD camp about the close relationship developing between Ebert and the old establishment in general, including the bureaucracy. By and large, this continued to function during the upheaval. For the USPD at least, here was additional evidence of the indifference of the majority of socialists to a radical overhaul of German society.

However, foreign-policy considerations also dictated Ebert's responses; he insisted that not to take action against the spread of extreme revolution in Germany would be to jeopardise the coming peace terms [107]. Ultimately, the SPD's co-operation with the army led to the bloody suppression of a Spartacist demonstration in Berlin on 6 December 1918. The alienation of the USPD from the provisional government was completed by their resignation from office on 29 December 1918 [*Doc. 2*].

In taking action to 'restore order' the old army was able to transmit some of its authority and most of its values to the Republic [*Doc. 18a*], incidentally frustrating the formation of a new 'People's Army'. Instead, the *Freikorps* (voluntary units), coming into being during the upheaval, responded to the command of the old army officers. Freed of the restraint of Haase and his USPD colleagues, SPD Minister of Defence, Gustav Noske, duly availed himself of the services of the *Freikorps* to crush the chaotic and badly organised Spartacist 'rising' in January 1919. The brutal murder of Liebknecht and Luxemburg on 15 January was a decisive enough answer to those few who wanted a Russian-style revolution in Germany [159; 162]. The exercise was repeated by these same forces – the basis of the new *Reichswehr* (Chapter 8) – in smashing the soviet that held sway briefly in Munich during April 1919 [53]. In sum, demands had clearly been widely voiced for measures of socialisation and demilitarisation during the revolution, suggesting that Ebert and the other SPD leaders *might* have made more of their opportunities. Yet the absence of any mass demand for sweeping revolution in Germany could not be overlooked. Anti-militarism was arguably more important than anti-capitalism – to judge from the tearing off of officers' insignia on the one hand and, on the other, the conciliatory agreements between employers and workers in December 1918 [44; 135]. The great German Congress of Workers' and Soldiers' Deputies, held in Berlin between 16 and 19 December 1918, endorsed Ebert's policy of preparing for elections to the National Assembly, thus decisively rejecting revolution.

Elections to the National Assembly took place on 19 January 1919. They represented a victory for parliamentary democracy that would have been inconceivable before the revolution. On the other hand, at a time when the harsh peace terms were not known and the prevailing mood made Berlin too dangerous to house the Assembly, which eventually met in Weimar (the city giving the Republic its name), the SPD did not win the absolute majority needed to implement even their programme. They had to rely on the support of the other two parties who were to make up the so-called 'Weimar coalition' – namely the Centre Party and the Democrats. The very appearance of these non-socialist parties, let alone the political organisations representing the powerful conservative forces of pre-war Germany, indicated the renewed confidence of those influential sectors of society that had been initially so overwhelmed by the revolution. The new Republic was forced from the outset to rest on a compromise between the very forces that had been in conflict within the German Empire [15; 26] Moreover, this compromise had been made possible in the last resort by the use of force. Yet some continuity was perfectly natural; the balance of power had at last been weighted by revolution in favour of the democratic mood that contemporaries like Gooch observed, and the compromise was, after all, enshrined in the constitution duly passed by the National Assembly after much debate on 31 July 1919.

Early drafts of the constitution were ready little more than a month after the outbreak of revolution. The views of its chief author, the Democrat Hugo Preuss, were modified by the arguments of the parties in the National Assembly through the twenty-eight member all-party committee chaired by another Democrat, Conrad Haussmann, as well as by the representations made by the various German states through the Committee of States set up on 25 January 1919. The responsible and meticulous discussion carried on in these committees and in the full Assembly ensured that the constitution, if a compromise, was neither a hasty nor an ill-considered arrangement [49]. Article 1 reaffirmed that power derived from the people and that the state was both a democracy and a republic. Sovereignty resided in the German parliament (Reichstag), which was to be elected every four years. In the post-war and post-revolutionary atmosphere the extension of the vote to men and women of twenty-one years of age was irresistible, even if this enfranchised politically immature and sometimes frankly hostile voters. The system of representation was proportional, whereby a party organisation drew up a list, for which people voted rather than for a specific local candidate. Each party was allocated one representative for every 60,000 votes cast in its favour. This did nothing to discourage the formation of smaller parties which, although they never attracted much support, contributed to making the system more volatile than it might otherwise have been [131].

The functions of the Reichstag can hardly be discussed without reference to the position of the Reich President. Notwithstanding the doubts in the SPD, the other political parties wanted the President to be able to act as a counterweight to the Reichstag. Thus, he was to be elected by a separate popular vote every seven years. In fact, this provision did not apply in the case of Friedrich Ebert, when he became the Republic's first President in August 1919. The controversial Article 48 of the constitution gave the President special powers to use in an emergency, but the Reichstag could reject any measures he proposed and his actions required the counter-signature of the Reich Chancellor. The President appointed the Reich Chancellor, who was responsible with his cabinet to parliament, and was empowered to dismiss him in the event of a no-confidence vote in the Reichstag. In view of the fateful use of the presidential authority during the crisis that brought Hitler to power, it is important to stress that there was no attempt at a presidential *coup d'état* during the lifetime of the Weimar Republic. The emergency powers of the President, on the other hand, were of use in difficult periods, for example in 1923 [3; 31]. How much weight should be attached to the belief that the use of presidential emergency powers positively encouraged the inclination of political parties to shun unpleasant and difficult duties is a matter for argument. Certainly, many Germans appeared to see the President as a sort of emperor-substitute and in regarding his office as a guarantee against parliamentary absolutism betrayed their own cynicism about democracy [15]. However, much depended, in the event, on the personality of the President, and there is some evidence to suggest that Ebert's reluctance to intervene in important political issues went to the point of actually weakening his office [51]. This is a reminder, useful even at this stage, that a number of factors interacting with each other affected the final outcome of the Republic, and the President's role will be reconsidered in due course.

The differing views on authority within the new Republic were bound to affect the complicated balance between central and local government. That much is clear from an examination of the second chamber set up by the constitution, the *Reichsrat*. Like its predecessor under the Bismarckian constitution, the *Bundesrat* (Federal Council), the new *Reichsrat* demonstrated the need of Weimar governments to reconcile themselves with the long and powerful tradition of separatism in Germany. The different German states strongly and successfully defended themselves against Preuss's original plans to readjust their boundaries, except for the case of Thuringia [23; 58]. At the same time, their federal association with the new Reich was no longer based, as it had been from 1871, on their existence as sovereign entities. Their designation under the new constitution as *Länder* (plural of *Land* – region) signified demotion from sovereign independence and thus the *Reichsrat*'s authority was also considerably curtailed. The latter continued to represent *Land* governments but was essentially, unlike the former *Bundesrat*, subservient to the Reichstag. Its most important power, that of vetoing the Reichstag's acts, could be overridden by a two-thirds vote in the 'lower' chamber. The attempt was made to prevent Prussia from dominating the *Reichsrat* by providing that no *Land* would be allowed more than two-fifths of the votes in the chamber. In addition, only half the Prussian votes were given to the Prussian government, with the remainder being distributed among the provinces of Prussia [18; 25].

The central government of the Reich therefore had considerable powers, and its laws took precedence over those of the various *Land* administrations. The constitution affirmed the Reich's control of foreign affairs, the armed forces and communications. Of particular importance was the supremacy of the central government in matters of taxation following the appointment of Matthias Erzberger as Minister of Finance in June 1919 [14; 55]. The enhanced control of the Reich was, on the other hand, offset to some extent by the considerable powers still residing with the *Länder*, notably in the sphere of police, the judiciary and education. There was therefore no absolute guarantee that a *Land* would not deliberately obstruct central government policies – for example in the case of Bavaria, where there was less respect for the Republic. The fact that Prussia still carried enormous weight helped partially to compensate for this, since it now became a stronghold of the Social Democrats [112].

In reviewing the constitution we have moved gradually from a consideration of the revolution to a survey of some of the problems facing the new Republic and which preoccupied the National Assembly. Of course, there were continuities in Germany's development before and after the revolution. Anti-democratic and anti-republican traits lived on within some of the German parties that resurfaced by early 1919. The German army retained something of its old influence; many, if not most, of the bureaucrats who drove the imperial administration remained in office; the plans for wide-ranging socialisation put forward by various councils for economic control had to be abandoned once the German socialists failed to secure their majority in the Reichstag. For all that, it would be reasonable to describe the finished constitution as a synthesis between, on the one hand, progressive political and social ideas and, on the other, the desire to protect traditional institutions. The second part of the constitution, elaborating the fundamental rights of German democracy, epitomised the scrupulous effort to be fair. Even if we accept that Ebert and his fellow socialists failed to capitalise on the advantages they enjoyed during the revolution, they apparently brought about a broadly acceptable outcome, in the sense that the constitution was eventually accepted by 262 to 75 votes. Outright opposition came only from the German Nationalists and the German People's Party. However, nothing would ever be the same again and even hostile forces had to operate within a new political framework. Legislation was only the beginning and, no matter what was 'put down on paper', the future would be determined by the specific challenges to the Republic and how it responded to them.

2 VERSAILLES: TRUTH AND FICTION

The peace treaty concluded between the German government and the Allied and Associated Powers at Versailles in 1919 provided the broad framework for the Weimar Republic's external relations. However, it also had major implications for the Republic's domestic harmony. The terms of peace were so objectionable to most Germans that how to react to the Versailles settlement, and thus how to conduct foreign policy, became a matter of prolonged and bitter dispute between German political parties [79]. Indeed, when the treaty provisions were finally transmitted officially to the Germans in draft form on 7 May 1919, the Republic's first parliamentary government under Philipp Scheidemann resigned rather than accept the peace terms. Yet Scheidemann's administration was based on the coalition of political forces that had captured three-quarters of the votes in the elections to the National Assembly, namely that between the SPD, the Democrats and the Centre Party – the so-called 'Weimar coalition'. Only when it became quite clear, even to the military leadership, that there was no possibility of resisting the Allied Powers by force, did a new SPD-Centrist coalition shoulder the burden of signing the peace treaty on 28 June, 1919. After heated debate on 22 and 23 June, no fewer than 138 votes in the National Assembly had been against authorising the government to sign. This protest, which included the Democrats and predictably the nationalists, was simply the most obvious indication of rejection and resentment experienced by the entire German population. Such was the mood that Ebert's election by popular vote, as mentioned earlier, had to be forgone in order to prevent the possible choice of a candidate from the right.

The disparity between the hostile reaction against the Versailles treaty in Germany and the way in which Weimar governments subsequently went on to adapt to and live with those terms as far as possible remains one of the most interesting features of the Republic's history. In that respect, the words 'truth and fiction' in this chapter's title describe the reaction of the German public. The popular mood was determined by fundamental, if mistaken, beliefs, not the least important being that Germany had fought the war for defensive purposes to avoid the threat of 'encirclement' by other powers before 1914 [59; 50]. Second, there was the assumption that the peace would be 'just' – that is to say based, on the celebrated Fourteen Points made by the American President Wilson in January 1918, which had been accepted in principle during the pre-Armistice negotiations in early November of that same year [101]. Third, it was thought that the proclamation of a Republic, with new forms of government and professedly new democratic values, made it even more necessary that Germany should not be treated in a punitive fashion.

Scheidemann's cabinet has often been castigated for failing to prepare the German public properly for disappointment with the peace terms. Yet German officials involved in the diplomatic exchanges long suspected that a harsh peace was likely. They had already realised during the Armistice preliminaries that the grim mood of the Allied leaders, themselves subject to domestic pressures to negotiate a harsh peace, did not promise an especially favourable *interpretation* of any of the main points at issue [85; 102]. Their pessimism was well founded. The Allied Powers eventually refused to invite the Germans to participate in the drafting of the peace terms, although this decision was also taken in order to save time and preserve Allied unity. For their part, the German government felt they had little option other than to press in any way they could for a favourable interpretation on key issues. This conviction guided the work of the enormous body of officials and experts in the special section set up in the German Foreign Office, who prepared a battery of written pleas and arguments for the attention of the peacemakers gathered in Paris [92]. In other words, German 'revisionism' dates less from the presentation of the actual treaty – which is the impression arising from countless descriptions of its shock impact – than from the very moment the Germans laid down their arms.

It is helpful to imagine a more or less continuous policy line running at least from November 1918 onwards, if not before, aimed at influencing the peace settlement in Germany's favour. Once engaged in this 'battle of the notes' the German leaders could hardly prepare the German public for a tough peace without undermining their entire strategy. The enforced signature of the treaty confirmed the worst of existing fears and underlined the need for a much more sustained and long-term campaign to modify the terms of peace.

Under these conditions it was essential even for the German government to stress that its signature was made under extreme protest. Furthermore, if the importance of precedent and wording in international agreements is acknowledged, then it is also possible to see more than senseless and 'nationalistic' protest in the concern of the German government to refute the notion of German 'responsibility' for the war implied in Article 231 of the Versailles treaty [*Doc. 4*] – the so-called 'war guilt' clause. That this process opened a gap between government and public awareness of the implications of the treaty was an unfortunate corollary of official tactics. However, it was possible to imagine that the gap might be narrowed in due course, in so far as the peace still had to be executed. Since this required Germany's co-operation there remained the hope of future bargaining.

This might not be immediately appreciated by a bald summary of the main peace terms as they stood on paper in 1919. The economic provisions of the treaty were, of course, deeply unwelcome and worrying to the Reich [155], as the famous economist Maynard Keynes argued almost too brilliantly, if not entirely accurately, in his book, *The Economic Consequences of the Peace* [138]. The impact of the reparations that were legally justified by Article 231 is discussed in Chapter 5, but other parts of the treaty were equally severe. Germany's overseas investments and property in enemy countries were confiscated, arguably more damaging than the enforced loss of her colonies. The capacity of Germany to promote its economic recovery through the resumption of its pre-war foreign trading was damaged by the compulsion to grant the Allied Powers most-favoured-nation treatment. This, together with the five-year ban on protective tariffs, affected the terms of any German trade agreements. The loss of resources in the detached territories in the east and the coal in the Saar region must naturally be placed on the debit side (Chapter 5). A reasoned rehearsal of the now familiar arguments for and against these provisions is superfluous, in that German public opinion could not be reached through such reasoning. It is, however, worth stressing firstly, that much depended on the future development of the German economy and the outcome of the reparations question; second, that Germany's economic attraction for East Europe was still considerable. That was most important, in view of the enormous interest throughout the whole of Europe in the early 1920s in opening up the Russian markets to western enterprise [65; 80].

Perhaps the territorial settlement at Versailles caused more immediate public resentment than reparations. In the west, Alsace-Lorraine was restored to France. Allied forces were to occupy the left bank of the Rhine for fifteen years, the withdrawal to take place in three stages of five years each [111]. Evacuation could be completed earlier if Germany fulfilled its treaty obligations and behaved. The left bank of the Rhine and the thirty-mile wide strip on the right bank were permanently demilitarised. The Saar was to be administered by the League of Nations for fifteen years, after which a plebiscite would determine its fate. Frontier adjustments were also made in favour of Belgium in Eupen, Malmedy and Moresnet, and in Denmark's favour, following a plebiscite, in North Schleswig [68]. On the eastern frontiers of Germany the fulfilment of number 13 of Wilson's Fourteen Points involved creating a corridor between East Prussia and the rest of the Reich to ensure that the new Polish state had 'secure access to the sea' via the port of Danzig. Thus, the provinces of Posen and West Prussia were handed over to Poland. Plebiscites in 1920 and 1921 left Germany in control of the disputed frontier districts of Marienwerder and Allenstein, as well as almost two-thirds of Upper Silesia [96]. If a million Germans thus fell under Polish rule, these were surrounded by areas predominantly settled by Poles. Moreover, Poland was not given the city of Danzig outright. Its German character was, in effect, acknowledged by making the port a free city under the supervision of a High Commissioner appointed by the League of Nations, whilst Poland supervised Danzig's foreign relations [89]. Less violently contested in Germany, until after 1933 at least, was the fate of the German minorities remaining in the areas ceded to Czechoslovakia. This was also broadly true of the loss of the German Baltic port at Memel to Lithuania, whose support the German government required against Poland [80]. In spite of German propaganda, it could be argued that the only outright violation of Wilson's professed ideal of self-determination over the German territorial settlement was the refusal of the Allies to permit the joining together of Austria and Germany [95; 109].

The arguments for and against the territorial readjustments have been given at prodigious length but, again, the Germans as a whole were unmoved by them. They felt injured, above all, by the shock of having to deal with the long-dominated and partitioned state of Poland as a great power in its own right once more [*Doc. 7b*]. Revision of the eastern frontiers was a policy which all Weimar governments and political parties were obligated to support. Although success in this endeavour seemed remote in 1919, there were a number of factors already working in Germany's favour. Not the least of these was the fact that the original French demands against Germany, which had included the annexation of the Rhineland and a far more generous treatment of the Polish claims, had been modified in response to Anglo-American pressure [62]. It was felt that if a less harsh line were not adopted on these issues then Germany might be driven to take more dangerous measures to revise its borders in the east. The Allies were also anxious that Germany remain strong enough to resist the possible, if greatly exaggerated, threat of communist infiltration of Central Europe [98].

France was made to feel more vulnerable when in 1920 the British-American guarantee of the Rhineland settlement lapsed, owing to the United States Senate's refusal to ratify the Versailles treaty. One outcome of this was that the French made more effort to offset their insecurity in the west by entering into close treaty arrangements with the newly formed states in the east, above all with Poland. Even so, in the long run the French were dependent on British support, and in East Europe the government in London was extremely reluctant to take on specific obligations, notwithstanding its great interest in ensuring stability in the region as a whole [62; 102]. Moreover, it was already plain that German economic influence, and therefore sooner or later political influence, would remain a major factor in the east, particularly since the peace conference failed to find a satisfactory answer to the problem of what to do about Russia. Within limits Germany could soon develop an active role in East Europe [*Doc. 7a*].

In total, Germany lost some 13 per cent of its territory and over six million subjects as a result of the Versailles settlement. It was generally a tough treaty, and France in particular, with an inferior population growth and comparatively weak industrial base, could be counted on to press for a strict interpretation of the peace terms. However, the French were unable to achieve this alone, in spite of Germany's undeniable military weakness after 1919 (Chapter 8). Weimar governments retained the possibility to work patiently and skilfully in their relations with foreign powers and 'to undertake the unavoidable in such a way as to derive the greatest possible credit for doing so' [7 *p. 43*] There remained, of course, the perennial problem for German statesmen of convincing internal opposition of the validity of this strategy, whilst the exclusion of the Republic from the League of Nations furnished extra ammunition for German nationalists railing against the peace *Diktat* [*Doc. 13*]. Rightist circles clearly had considerable success in propagating the false notion that the 'unjust' peace need not have been signed in the first place. To accept this demanded, incredibly enough, a belief that, in spite of the mass revulsion against war which had nurtured the revolution, Germany had not been militarily defeated; that it could have fought on, had the army not been 'stabbed in the back' by the politicians.

The logic of this approach was to focus nationalist resentment not on the foreign victors but on the 'November criminals' who had initiated the Armistice talks [198; 211]. By implication, this condemned any individuals or parties who believed in the necessity of revising the peace terms through collaboration with the former enemy powers. The Versailles treaty certainly did not doom the Republic from birth, but it *did* create particularly troublesome dimensions to existing internal conflicts and contradictions which had, to some extent, survived the revolution [19; 39]. The best way to demonstrate this is to examine some of the fundamental problems of the Weimar Republic before turning to the final crisis to see how the complex interaction of many factors brought Hitler to power.

PART TWO: PROBLEMS

3 COALITIONS AND PARTY POLITICS

The limited nature of the changes wrought by the revolution was emphasised by the confident reappearance in the National Assembly of the pre-war political parties. Henceforth German cabinets – and with them efficient government – were dependent on coalitions. What this meant, in effect, was that the unresolved structural crisis of Wilhelmine Germany was carried over into the post-war era and social conflicts were renewed in the parliaments of the Republic. This intrinsic weakness predisposed German party politics towards selfish battles of interests which were likely, in turn, to exaggerate the severity of any internal or external crisis facing the Republic [133]. It remains all the more important to emphasise the greatly changed context in which inter-party disputes were renewed. The location of sovereignty in the Reichstag meant that at last political conflicts could be continued right up to government level. This process often resulted in hesitant and fitful policy but it could at least build to a limited extent on what party political development had taken place in the later stages of the German Empire. Mistakes were inevitable but this was an unavoidable part of the learning curve for Weimar democracy. It is appropriate to consider in the first instance those parties which were, at least in principle, committed to evolving within the new order and consolidating the Republic – namely the Centre Party, the SPD, the Democrats (*Deutsche Demokratische Partei* – DDP) and the German People's Party (*Deutsche Volkspartei* – DVP). By and large, these political parties were responsible for the constructive policies developed during the Republic's lifetime.

The four parties shared, or at least came to share for a period, a commitment to preserving the Republic. This was self-evident in the case of the SPD [112; 122] but also clearly expressed by the DDP, founded on 25 November 1918 from the old Progressive Party and the left wing of the National Liberals [116; 124]. The new formation aimed to rally the bourgeois liberal, intellectual forces of pre-war Germany to the new order [*Doc. 5*]. The Centre Party

(*Zentrumspartei*), established in 1870, was hostile towards the revolution and at first not actively in favour of the new Republic. However, it did share with the SPD a long-standing interest in parliamentary developments in Wilhelmine Germany. Moreover, its extremely diverse social composition predisposed it towards compromise within the new Republic, particularly since its left wing had been strengthened under Matthias Erzberger as a result of the war [14; 132]. Its advocacy of centralised government in the Reich brought it into sharp conflict with its sister Catholic party, the Bavarian People's Party (*Bayerische Volkspartei* – BVP), but the two forces invariably combined over the all-important defence of the Catholic church, culture and education matters [114]. The DVP, on the other hand, was a conservative party founded by Gustav Stresemann and Hugo Stinnes from the right wing of the old National Liberals in late November 1918. Initially hostile to the Republic, monarchist and anti-socialist, the DVP was increasingly influenced by Stresemann towards working within the Republican state form after the excesses of 1919–22 and the economic and monetary collapse in Germany in 1923 [123; 126; 134].

The years between 1919 and 1923 witnessed rightist and leftist risings, political assassinations on a large scale and a frightening economic collapse. The new style of coalition governments was bound to be tested to near destruction in the face of countless unpopular and harsh decisions. Moreover, the public discontent in the post-war years soon manifested itself in the well-known swing towards political extremes. Whereas, for example, the 'Weimar coalition' of SPD-Centre Party-DDP had been supported by three-quarters of the electorate in the polls for the National Assembly, it could win the support of only a minority of electors in the battle for seats in the first Reichstag in June 1920 [*Doc. 6*]. One indicator of the alarming difficulties in the way of formulating and carrying out consistent policies was that the four parties so far mentioned were variously involved in no fewer than nine administrations between February 1919 and the close of 1923. On the surface, this appears to substantiate the gloomy criticism that only between 1923 and 1929 was it feasible to speak of parliamentary government in Germany in any meaningful way [133].

Nonetheless, many of the same political figures were involved in the re-shuffles. Moreover, Article 48 turned out to be a stabilising factor, and from the turmoil came, in the end, some worthy achievements. Not the least of these was progress towards economic reconstruction and the resolution of some thorny foreign-policy issues (Chapters 4 and 5). Equally important, the constant struggle against extremism provided invaluable experience to the coalition parties, in the sense that the crises strengthened the determination of those politicians who were struggling to make the most of what opportunities existed for constructive action. This development could be traced in the climactic formation of the 'Great Coalition' during the appalling crisis of 1923, when Stresemann's first cabinet was based on the SDP, DDP, Centre Party and his own DVP. Ultimately, and for all the 'first uneasy groping for their new role' [131], the four parties in question could not wholly eliminate essential differences between them. Indeed, these tended to become more pronounced with the passing of the crisis and the more indulgent mood engendered by the atmosphere of relative well-being during the years between 1924 and 1928 [121].

Ideological conflicts between political parties are not, of course, incompatible with sound government, and parliamentary experience did continue to make progress between the economic crisis of 1923 and the far more severe one of 1929. Success in this direction remained qualified by the ultimate failure of the respective parties to strike a proper balance between the socio-economic interests which they represented and the interests of the state [*Doc. 19*]. Arguably, this confirmed simply that much more time, trial and error was needed for the parties to escape from the bad habits and practices of Wilhelmine Germany and to grow into the responsibilities of their new roles. Yet criticism of the parliamentary system has also been based on the alleged dearth of positive and forceful leadership in the major parties. Somewhat unfairly, the SPD leadership was also charged with compounding its failure to exploit its position during the revolution by going on to a process of 'continuous error'. The SPD did not succeed in transforming their initial association with the bourgeois parties, or so-called 'democratic middle' of DDP, Centre Party and DVP, into a lasting and constructive partnership, even though the Social Democrats had jettisoned their left wing and could never expect to gain support from the nationalist right. By the end of 1923 the SPD leaders had opted out of direct governmental responsibility, and the party reverted to its 'habit of opposition'. It did not re-enter the government until 1928 [112; 130].

There were admittedly some particularly difficult factors working against the SPD leadership. It tended to depend on the trade-union movement, and this limited its political manoeuvrability to a degree. Also, the SPD increasingly found itself forced, in the face of widespread socio-economic distress, to compete for votes with the

German Communist Party (KPD). The KPD made inroads among the militant, young and unemployed elements of German society [20; 34]. Whilst the reunification of the USPD and the SPD in 1922 testified to the growing concern of the socialist movement to protect the interests of the German working class [168], the decision to abandon the bourgeois coalitions was almost certainly a tactical error. It can be argued that a better, more effective, if less popular, route to protect the interests for which the SPD stood, and to counter the attractions of the KPD, would have been to remain in government. Within this, the German socialists should have been able to continue pressing for more attractive and constructive solutions to a range of issues facing Germany in the second half of the 1920s. In opposition the SPD nonetheless continued to support the political values of the Republic and provided backing for the government of the day as far as it could in a responsible fashion. Many regretted that this was still far from the most satisfactory way to exploit the impressive mass basis of the SPD. Until 1932 it remained the largest party in the Reichstag.

The above developments affected to some extent the internal condition of the three political parties which, without the SPD, formed five of the seven administrations between 1924 and the end of June 1928 (the other two cabinets included the German National People's Party, *Deutsch-nationale Volkspartei* – DNVP). Both the Centre Party and the DDP had a pronounced inclination to distrust socialist policies – less those that aimed at the improvement of working-class conditions than measures which threatened private property. This reservation applied, of course, with greater force to the DVP, which was in effect 'the parliamentary mouthpiece of industry' [31]. The readiness of both the Centrist and DVP leadership to co-operate with the rightist DNVP was therefore more in evidence after 1923. During that year the transformation of Stresemann, to responsible party leader and 'republican by conviction' (*Vernunftrepublikaner*) was completed. His growing determination to bring stability to Germany could be seen in his efforts to hold together the 'Great Coalition' on which his government rested, following his appointment as Chancellor in August 1923.

Stresemann's achievement in persuading his party, together with the Centre Party, DDP and SPD, to accept the unpopular decision to end passive resistance in the Ruhr, was quite remarkable. He professed his commitment to continuing the middle-of-the-road policies in the interests of Germany's existence. 'I regard it as my duty, as a party man and minister, to do all I can to unite the

German people for these decisions, and not to force upon them the choice: bourgeois or socialist' [134 *p. 164*]. Naturally, the SPD's defection from government intensified Stresemann's problems. To make matters worse, the elections of 4 May 1924 appeared to confirm that voters had little interest in the courageous achievement of stabilisation and currency reform (Chapter 5). The DVP, DDP and SPD all lost supporters, whereas the DNVP was able to reap the rewards of opposition to unpopular policies by becoming the second largest party in the Reichstag [*Doc. 6*]. Those critics of Stresemann within the DVP were more resolved to try to bring the nationalists into government, where they would have to shoulder their share of responsibility, taking some of the sting out of the virulent rightist opposition to the Republic and its policies. There appeared to be some hope of bringing this about after 1923, in spite of the way in which the DNVP had conducted itself after 1919 [188; 219] (Chapter 7). The power balance was such that from 1923 successful coalition performances relied on making concessions either to the left or right, or both – or even, given the SPD's decision to remain in opposition, including the nationalists in the government. This is what happened under Chancellor Luther in 1925 and Chancellor Marx in 1927.

The prevailing conditions, therefore, hardly encouraged the subjugation of party interests to those of the state, but there were tantalising vistas of better things to come. Not surprisingly, Stresemann was an important factor once more. After his brief Chancellorship came to an end, he remained Foreign Minister for the next six years and his work in this office helped to bring some coherence to the political forces represented in the Reichstag. On the whole, his foreign policy was backed by the SPD and the trade unions, as well as the moderate bourgeois parties, the DDP and the Centre Party. Admittedly, Stresemann's diplomacy never won the total support of his own party, let alone the DNVP, but by insisting on the 'primacy' of foreign affairs Stresemann aimed over time to exploit his diplomatic successes and his active trade policy to bring about a greater degree of cohesion in the Reichstag. Specifically, he hoped to leave the nationalists little option other than to support his diplomacy. The DNVP was, after all, divided over the Dawes Plan (Chapter 7), with its important economic pressure groups favouring the new reparations deal. At any rate, the German conservatives were persuaded to remain in government long enough for the Locarno treaties to be negotiated [125]. The right's renewed and bitter campaigns against the Locarno policies thereafter did not, as long as Stresemann stayed in office and his international reputation remained high, bring the DNVP any tangible benefits [*Doc. 9*].

It remained much more difficult for the parties of the middle to prosecute consistent domestic policies, thus also making it harder to counter the incessant propaganda from both right and left [127; 128]. Trade unions, for example (even the Christian trade unions affiliated to the 'loyal' Centre Party), were bent on resisting legislation over wages or the length of the working day – areas where DVP interests were particularly keen on introducing change. On the other hand, the DVP's commitment to developing maximum exports appeared to be at odds with the effort made by the powerful agrarian interests behind the DNVP (Chapter 7) to reintroduce protective tariffs in order to counter the attraction of cheap agricultural imports. This blatant attempt to keep food prices higher for the benefit of German farmers was naturally opposed by working-class interest groups too. In short, whilst there was some possibility of compromise between the parties in the centre and the two parliamentary 'wings', the DNVP and the SPD, co-operation rarely went beyond tactical alliances for specific purposes. These developments, it has been argued, 'had little permanence in view of the deep ideological and socio-economic rifts which the class conflict, accentuated by the reparations question and the distribution of its financial burdens, produced in the Reichstag' [31 *p. 77*].

The zigzag course of policy-making which this state of affairs entailed did indeed do much to discredit the notion of parliamentary government among the German public at large. The latter became disillusioned by the rigidity of the party organisations and principles and discouraged by the horse-trading which accompanied the formation of each new coalition government [115; 124]. It proved to be exceedingly difficult to evolve stable cabinet traditions, since ministers were often at the mercy of inter-party disputes and of the whims of their own parliamentary factions. The development of a proper working relationship between government and legislature thus remained fitful, as was shown by the occasional device of a cabinet of above-party 'experts' or personalities (Chapter 9). That, of course, encouraged sceptics to see promise only in the President's powers and in the day-to-day continuity of the work of the bureaucracy. That party leaders were only too well aware of the dangers can be seen from the plans for reform which were proposed at various times and which tried to define more suitably the role that parties should play in the processes of government [3; 5; 15], a subject on which the constitution had been suitably vague.

Of interest, however, to the historian looking for the might-have-beens of the Republic is that the easy ridicule of the Weimar parliamentary system by extremist parties, as well as the press organs, obscured the elements of promise, already briefly mentioned, which a more dispassionate observer of the scene might have found. It detracted from the constant and unfailing effort of German Social Democracy to keep alive the values of the Republic. It minimised the importance of the continuous presence and effort in the coalitions of the DVP and Centre Party, which helped to compensate for the continuing decline of German liberalism – marked in the original split between DVP and DDP in 1918 and in the continuing election losses of the DDP thereafter. It undervalued the contribution of the Centre Party's efforts to go beyond a strictly confessional basis and to bridge party differences by attempting to work with the DNVP at the national level and with the Social Democrats in the largest *Land*, Prussia. Such important and interesting elements of *rapprochement* should not be pushed aside by hindsight. They did something at least to counter the historic tendency of German parties since 1848 to splinter into factional interests: a trend taken to absurdity in the growth of even smaller, powerless yet confusing parties (such as the German Business Party) from 1 per cent in 1919 to 8 per cent in 1930 [124]. The painful progress towards parliamentary maturity after 1918 must also be judged in the light of extremist efforts on the right and left to discredit the Republican institutions. Thus, if it is indeed permissible to see in the behaviour of political leaders and parties after 1929 the outcome of earlier flaws and errors, it is equally vital to stress the quite extraordinary nature of the years between 1929 and 1933.

4 FOREIGN POLICY

For most Germans, foreign policy meant a continuous and unremitting effort to revise the terms of the Treaty of Versailles, but if the end was agreed the means were not, and the conduct of foreign relations played its part in intensifying party political disputes. Admittedly, all shades of political opinion saw some virtue during the early years 1919–23 in being obstructive about the execution of the terms which officially came into force on 10 January 1920 – hence the effective avoidance of the clauses demanding action against the Kaiser and war criminals, the defiant German propaganda to disprove the charges of war guilt, the temporising of German governments over the demands to dismantle the paramilitary organisations, and the outright hostility shown towards the various Allied control commissions watching over the implementation of the peace terms [59].

Yet the mood of resistance was matched by the greater determination of the Allies, and of France in particular, to end German prevarication. On 5 May 1921 the Allied London Ultimatum called firmly for the proper execution of the treaty terms and in particular for the acceptance by Germany of the new schedule for reparations payments (Chapter 5). Since three Rhine ports had already been occupied by the Allies on 8 March 1921, the point was taken, none the less courageously, by the new Chancellor from the Centre Party, Joseph Wirth, who in his two administrations, between 10 May 1921 and late November 1922, developed the policy of 'fulfilment'. The policy was a necessary expedient, based on the premise that to show determined good faith in trying to carry out the peace terms properly would not only demonstrate how impossible a task this was, but would therefore also induce the Allied Powers to be more lenient in interpreting the treaty [129].

Wirth's strategy was supported in general by the 'Weimar coalition', but was bitterly opposed by the nationalists [Doc. 14]. The violence of the mood engendered by extremist reactions expressed itself in the murder in August 1921 of Matthias Erzberger (the German representative on the Armistice Commission in November 1918). The success of any attempt to counteract the appeal of nationalist criticism therefore depended in part on the policy of fulfilment bringing quick results. Yet the intractable nature of the reparations problems precluded rapid progress, and after Wirth's resignation in November 1922 the 'business ministry' of Dr Wilhelm Cuno was left to face French action in the Ruhr in 1923, making the German nationalists only too happy with their country's policy of 'passive resistance' against the Allies (Chapter 5) [152].

Wirth cannot be judged without looking also at his government's contribution to the development of Germany's relations with Soviet Russia. Much attention has been lavished on the 'Unholy Alliance' [72] of defeated Germany and a Russia that was politically ostracised by the West's aversion to Bolshevism. In fact, co-operation between the two 'outcasts' rested firmly on the basis of mutual self-interest and was never an 'alliance' in any formal sense. Firstly, the German demand for new markets was matched by the desperate need of the weakened Soviet state for foreign aid and capital investment. Second, the vast spaces of Russia, inaccessible to the Allied Control Commission, offered hope for Germany's future secret development of military weapons and techniques [138]. Third, the prospects seemed good for a revival of the traditional German-Russian co-operation against the Polish state. Russia had lost territories to Poland by the Treaty of Riga in March 1921; both Russia and Germany were hostile to the fact that in the French system of alliances Poland was allotted a central role in forming a 'barrier' of states between them. In short, Soviet Russia could apparently hasten Germany's return to great-power status by helping to develop Germany's economic and military potential [93].

Moreover, since the Russians were not bound by any peace treaty with the Allies, they could theoretically initiate diplomatic moves in Germany's interests but for the moment outside Germany's power. This became a very real possibility when the Red Army seemed on the verge of defeating Poland in 1920 [83]. So striking were these prospects to key economic thinkers, to military leaders like Seeckt (Chapter 8), and to men like Baron Ago von Maltzan, head of the Russian department of the German Foreign Office (*Auswärtiges Amt*), that they argued strongly in favour of developing good relations with Russia at the earliest possible moment [*Doc. 7b*]. Seeckt authorised preliminary contacts with the Russians with a view to military collaboration after his meeting with Karl Radek, Lenin's agent in Berlin, in early January 1920. In 1920, too, unofficial German-Russian economic contacts at private level steadily increased. The resumption of normal German-Soviet relations, which would entail recognition of Soviet Russia, was, however, a political step of the first importance and ran the risk of alienating the Allied Powers [26; 79].

The response of the German political leadership to Russia's overtures was therefore more cautious. Under foreign ministers like Adolf Köster in 1920 and Walther Simons in the early part of 1921, German-Russian relations were not permitted to develop too quickly. Typically, the German-Soviet provisional commercial agreement of 6 May 1921, though far more important, was not signed until the British government had taken a similar step [72]. The policy of fulfilment launched by Wirth would have been less credible had it been accompanied by obviously closer ties with Russia, but the fact remains that not only was Wirth in favour of a more active eastern policy, in part because of his own dislike of Poland, but that in 1921 conditions favoured this. The introduction in Russia of Lenin's New Economic Policy (NEP), which opened the way to the limited return of some private enterprise, provided an improved environment for German investment there. Furthermore, in the calculations of the Allied Reparations Commission (Chapter 5), Russia appeared to retain the option of exercising the right (theoretically due to her according to Article 116 of the Versailles treaty) to claim war damages against Germany. It was unlikely that this would arise, in view of Lenin's attack on the 'robber peace' of Versailles, but the situation might be changed in the event of closer relations between Russia and the Allies. It was therefore in Wirth's interest not to let the policy of fulfilment lead to a worsening of German-Russian relations [129]. Unlike Seeckt, for example, the political leaders tried hard to keep open both options, East and West. Pressure on Wirth to commit himself to the Russian connection intensified, firstly as the outcome of the plebiscite over Silesia in 1921 further inflamed German opinion against the Poles, and second as the reparations crisis developed. On forming his second administration, Wirth encouraged the more active phase of the secret German-Russian exchanges which, after stops and starts, produced the Rapallo agreement between Germany and Russia, signed on 16 April 1922 during the World Economic Conference at Genoa [71]. A study of this treaty's implications throws light generally on early Weimar diplomacy.

In the first place, the agreement was signed only after it had become fairly clear that, especially given the hard line towards

Germany of the new French leader, Poincaré, Germany could expect few concessions at the Genoa conference over the Versailles terms, in particular those relating to reparations. Even the German Foreign Minister, Walther Rathenau, whose name had been associated with fulfilment and who valued close work with the Allied Powers, acknowledged this [79; 91]. In the second place, the Russians had, in effect, made it clear that they did not accept the premises on which the Genoa conference was held. This was the first post-war conference to include the Russians, and Lloyd George's dream of a restored European economy involved a plan for a world consortium at Genoa to exploit Russian trade. On political grounds, however, the Bolsheviks preferred to concentrate on securing close economic ties with individual countries, particularly Germany, and they were not above playing on German fears about Article 116 to achieve their end. In the event, the Rapallo agreement shattered the conference and confirmed the worst fears of the French about German-Russian retaliation against Versailles.

Yet, arguably, the French would have continued to take a hard line towards Germany in any event and the Rapallo agreement did not in the least mean that German foreign policy would now be chiefly concerned with Russia. Admittedly, it put the Poles under greater pressure by emphasising their exposed position [63], and historians seem to be agreed that the pact marked the beginning of a greater freedom of movement for German policy-makers, giving them a useful lever in their dealings with the Allied Powers [92]. Yet these were more psychological advantages, not to be found in the text of the agreement, which merely disposed of the bogey of Article 116, since the two powers mutually renounced claims for war damages, provided for the resumption of normal diplomatic relations and opened the way for an intensification of economic contacts by promising each other most-favoured-nation treatment. These arrangements in fact mirrored the sort of economic agreements which Berlin had been negotiating with the Baltic countries since the end of 1919 [*Doc. 7a*]. In this respect the Rapallo agreement must also be seen in the light of Germany's effort to consolidate its position in eastern Europe. The pact operated on many levels. If a threat to Poland and the Franco-Polish *rapprochement* could be read into the agreement, on the other hand, it acted in the long run like a magnet to the smaller eastern European states by providing one of the few constants in a confused period. It suggested that their own future welfare lay in playing an accommodating role in the development of German-Russian

economic contacts rather than becoming enmeshed in alliances
against these two powers.

All parties except one in Germany reacted favourably to the
implication that the Rapallo agreement was an important step on
the way to Germany's recovery, nationalists conveniently over-
looking the difference in ideologies between the republic and the
world's first communist state. Such differences, of course, earned the
'Rapallo policy' the dislike of the SPD [*Doc. 7c*], whose leaders
feared an increase in KPD influence. Neither did the German
socialists wish to alienate Allied opinion. Yet the events of 1923,
when France invaded the Ruhr, simply confirmed what Wirth and
all other realists knew, that the useful German-Russian connection
could never be an end in itself. During the inflationary and political
crisis of 1923 the Russo-German 'alliance' helped to remove the
threat of possible simultaneous Polish action in the East to complement the French invasion of the Ruhr [105]. It could solve
neither the reparations crisis nor the other problems of Versailles, as
Wirth's double-edged policies had shown. In this sense, Stresemann
benefited from his predecessors' efforts, and it is not surprising that
the Ruhr crisis contributed to the process of 'liberating Stresemann
from the views of a narrow, conservative partisan politician' [64;
74].

Stresemann, who became Chancellor for a brief period beginning
in August and thereafter dominated German policy as Foreign
Minister until his death in 1929, followed the aims of all previous
German officials in seeking to revise the Versailles treaty. Whether
one accepts that his policy was a variation on the 'fulfilment'
policies of Wirth, in its attention to both the East and West, or
whether one believes that his emphasis on 'partial revision' was
quite novel, attention must be given to the vastly changed circumstances in which Stresemann was able to operate [94; 99]. Of the
greatest importance, the shocking social and economic effects of the
Ruhr crisis had prepared the Allies to consider Germany's
difficulties more carefully [62]. This was seen at its most striking in
the replacement of the discredited Poincaré by the new French
leader, Edouard Herriot, who was in principle prepared to co-
operate with Germany. Yet the French, with their inferiority in
numbers and industrial potential, still needed security against a
future resurgent Germany, particularly since the restraining effect of
the Rapallo pact on Poland in 1923 had thrown into grave doubt
the usefulness of France's eastern allies. Hence the importance of
Stresemann's recognition of the need for conciliatory moves towards

France, and in ending passive resistance in the Ruhr he also demonstrated his 'courage to be unpopular'. [134; *p. 119*].

Economic stability and the resolution of Germany's currency problems were absolutely essential prerequisites for the success of Stresemann's policy (Chapter 5), for these provided the more normal conditions for lengthy diplomatic exchanges. Thus, by 1925 Stresemann was at last in a position to reopen an idea which Chancellor Cuno had raised prematurely in 1922, that of a security pact with the Allied Powers. Such a pact was achieved with the conclusion of the Locarno treaties in October 1925 and their eventual signature in London on 1 December 1925. These were agreements pivotal to Stresemann's whole policy [84; 88]. The Locarno settlement provided for an outright acceptance by Germany of her western borders, those with Belgium and France, and mutual guarantees to this effect were to enter into force (as were the other arrangements for the East) when Germany became a member of the League of Nations [*Doc. 8*]. This arrangement went at least some way to relieve France of anxiety about her borders with Germany and opened the field for greater co-operation between Germany, France and Britain. There is thus a fairly clear line running from Locarno. In December 1925 the Allies evacuated the first occupation zone on the left bank of the Rhine (Chapter 2); in the autumn of 1926 Germany entered the League of Nations, hitherto dominated by France and Britain, which also gave the Republic new opportunities to further its policies of support for German minorities abroad [69; 70]; in the summer of 1927 the Allies agreed to reduce their Rhineland occupation forces by 10,000. By 1929 the 'Young Plan' had been put into action (Chapter 9) and an early evacuation of the Rhineland was on the cards.

If these achievements helped to pull together the moderate parties (Chapter 3), the Locarno treaties were bitterly disliked by the German nationalists, as was any co-operation with the detested League of Nations, and thus, ultimately, Stresemann was deprived of complete victory even over his own party [75; 134]. This is the more regrettable in that Stresemann also made considerable efforts to convince public opinion in Germany of the need for a much longer time-scale in revising the eastern borders of the Reich. In sharp contrast to his guarantee of Germany's western borders, Stresemann would sign only treaties of arbitration with Czechoslovakia and Poland, thus creating a precedent for the different treatment of the peace settlement in East and West, a more important step in the quest for revisionism than any yet taken [52; 75]. This success would have been inconceivable without the changed European atmosphere after 1923, although it also reflected Britain's aversion to extending its commitments to eastern Europe, which made matters easier for Stresemann [84].

Just as Rapallo had not precluded keeping open options with the West, so Locarno did not mean entirely closing options in the East with Russia. When Germany entered the League it was relieved of the obligation to take up arms against Russia in the event of conflict between that country and another state (Poland for example!) in accordance with the obligations imposed by Article 16 of the League Covenant. In a note from Great Britain and France to Germany it was agreed at Locarno that a League member could only fulfil its obligations to the League under Article 16 (which provided for sanctions against an aggressor) to the extent 'compatible with its military and geographical situation'. In effect, this meant a recognition by the Allied Powers of the special relationship which existed between Russia and Germany [67]. Thus, once the Locarno agreements had been safely negotiated – and not a moment before, in spite of Russian pressure – Stresemann continued to develop the long-standing contacts with Moscow by signing the Treaty of Berlin in April 1926. It provided for continuing mutual good relations between the two powers, clarified Germany's stand *vis-à-vis* Article 16, and opened the way for further large German credits to Russia [72].

Locarno and Berlin, taken together, show not so much a balancing act as the fact that 'East' or 'West' could never individually satisfy Germany's needs after the Versailles treaty had been signed [*Doc. 8*]. In many ways Stresemann simply made more explicit trends in Weimar diplomacy between 1919 and 1923, for the striking feature of that diplomacy at the level of departmental officialdom was its realism [92]. Realism reached, so to speak, a new peak under Stresemann, as can be seen by glancing finally at the *cause célèbre* of German nationalists, Poland and its relations with Germany after Locarno. In effect, these pacts excluded any effort at a forceful revision of the Polish-German frontiers, an illusion of German nationalists given Germany's military weakness. The Locarno treaties did not, of course, preclude economic pressure on Poland, as could be seen by the Polish-German trade war after 1925. In this sense the continuing links between Moscow and Berlin remained invaluable, although the improving international climate no· longer threw Germany and Russia so closely together and the likelihood of them collaborating against Poland and the border states was virtually nil [92]. There is now, moreover, a great deal of evidence to suggest that, in spite of the inevitable and continuing stress on revisionism against Poland at the level of 'high policy', at the lower level of everyday negotiations – for example over each country's minorities – there was a real effort in Berlin and Warsaw to find a *modus vivendi* in the changed atmosphere after Locarno [105; 106; 110].

It is impossible to say where these developments would have led, since they depended to a great extent on the ability of foreign ministers to manage the ever present pressures of their domestic opponents. The force of Stresemann's personality and the weight of his reputation made it possible for Germany to develop a consistent foreign policy between 1923 and 1929 in spite of such pressures. Such was the penalty of Versailles that, if it left open room for movement, it remained the easy target for nationalist propaganda and prevented Stresemann from getting full credit for his remarkable policies. These promised to strike an acceptable balance between German and European interests in the long run. Sadly, Stresemann's death in 1929 coincided with an economic crisis during which the sort of national feelings were aroused that made it even more difficult to achieve a compromise at any level.

5 ECONOMICS AND REPARATIONS

Although the Weimar Republic's early economic difficulties were not primarily caused by the reparations issue, the ill-feeling engendered by this problem produced the sort of uncertainty which was bound to aggravate existing economic difficulties. As a result of an economy isolated by wartime conditions, the supply of goods in Germany did not keep pace with the natural increase in paper money, and excess purchasing power, not absorbed by higher taxes, pushed up prices. The abandonment of the gold standard in Germany on 4 August 1914 removed another restriction on the issue of currency, and thus inflation was pronounced before the war ended. In 1914 a dollar was worth 4.29 marks; by early 1920, 100 marks. The shock was greater when in 1919 Germany was again exposed to wider economic contacts and the relative scarcity of goods and raw materials resulting from the war effort brought further price increases.

The lost resources of the German territories handed over at Versailles included 14.6 per cent of arable land, 74.5 per cent of iron ore, 68.1 per cent of zinc ore, 26 per cent of coal production as well as the potash mines and textile industries of Alsace. Other losses included merchant ships over 1,600 gross tons, half the merchant ships between 1,000 and 1,600 gross tons, a quarter of the fishing fleet, large quantities of rail locomotives and rolling stock as well as any public property in the ceded territories and colonies, armaments (Chapter 8) and finally German property in Allied territories. The Republic was saddled with a colossal debt incurred from financing the war of some 150 milliard marks, whilst post-war difficulties in Germany demanded government expenditure on an unprecedented scale [155]. It is in such a context that the reparations problem must be examined.

The Versailles treaty left open the amount to be paid by Germany in reparations to meet the civilian war damages claims of the Allies, and the task of determining Germany's total indebtedness was carried out in the Inter-Allied Reparations Commission. This began its work on 10 January 1920 and continued through various conferences of the Allied leaders. Meanwhile, Germany was to make large deliveries of gold, convertible currency, goods and raw materials. By 27 April 1921, the Commission had set the total of Germany's debt at 132 milliard gold marks. Following the London Ultimatum of 5 May 1921, and in accordance with the concept of 'fulfilment' (Chapter 4), Wirth's government made the first large cash payments in August 1921 [146]. The rapid inflation which had set in in Germany after the London Ultimatum continued, however, and at the end of 1921 the German government declared itself unable to make the payments due for 15 January and 15 February 1922.

It was already clear to most people by this time that reparations were as much a political as an economic issue – hence Lloyd George's ambitious plans for a solution in the wider context of a regeneration of the whole European economy and the convening of the World Economic Conference at Genoa [156]. America's understandable concern for the repayment of its loans to the Allied Powers was another factor, impelling the latter, however, to press Germany harder for reparations. In addition, the attitude of the French in particular hardened over the reparations issue after the shock of the Rapallo agreement. The Allied case was that it was in Germany's power to effect reforms of her currency and taxation and to stabilise the mark in order to achieve the budgetary surplus for reparations payments. In effect, this was to assume that it was deliberate German policy to allow an economic and financial crisis in order to escape unwelcome burdens. Poincaré seized the chance to test these views when, in some desperation, he ordered the occupation of the Ruhr in January 1923, following a technical default of German payments in kind, and prepared to force the Reich to accept its responsibilities over reparations.

The German government's case was that reparations had intensified, if not caused, its economic difficulties and that some agreement was needed before Germany could control her spiralling inflation. The Germans had in mind a moratorium on payments and a foreign loan. Two important points arise here. Firstly, whilst the 'non-party' government of Wilhelm Cuno proclaimed Germany's inability to meet reparations charges, they responded to the French occupation of the Ruhr by ordering 'passive resistance', and this cost Germany more than twice the annual charge of reparations which it declared itself unable to make in 1921 [152]. Second, the Germans stabilised their currency prior to a settlement being agreed over reparations and before receiving a foreign loan. After Stresemann's courageous ending of passive resistance on 26 September 1923 a new currency was issued on 15 November 1923, the so-called *Rentenmark*. The crucial question was how far this would command confidence in Germany, since currency needs to be 'covered' and the Reich no longer had sufficient reserves of gold and foreign currency [150]. An ingenious answer was the founding of the *Rentenbank*, which was endowed with collateral in the form of mortgages on all land used by industry and agriculture. This solution sufficed until the printing of a new Reichsmark at the end of August 1924, and with the circulation of money bought under strict control the German government no longer relied, as it had tended to, on the printing presses of the *Reichsbank*.

These events appeared to substantiate charges of German duplicity. Critics rightly pointed out that financial experts like the President of the *Reichsbank*, Rudolf Haverstein, had made the post-war inflation worse by being too liberal with the issue of credit before the 'collapse' of 1923 [153]. With some justice, German industrialists and speculators were accused of profiting from inflation, but the failure of the German government to take properly firm action before 1923 can be more reasonably explained by seeing men like Wirth as the victims to some extent of the magnitude and novelty of post-war economic problems [151]. One only has to examine misguided efforts by German governments to carry out tax reforms before 1923, even if there is truth in the charge that they feared alienating the right, to see how inadequately suited were older conceptions to the changed conditions. What use was it, for example, defining taxes in terms of nominal money value at a time of progressive currency depreciation? [155] Moreover, the stabilisation of the currency came after Germany had endured a traumatic crisis and when the need for unpopular decisions was demonstrably clear. This factor is not generally sufficiently stressed – although admittedly the German leaders had to justify policies to parties and pressure groups who treated the Versailles terms as unwarrantable.

Finally, it has to be recognised that Germany's internal solution to its inflationary crisis in 1923 was a temporary one and depended on further arrangements at an international level. That was recognised when, in October 1923, the American President, Calvin Coolidge, supported the proposals leading to a new plan for reparations which took its name from the chairman of a committee of experts, Charles Dawes. The Dawes Plan, in force from 1 September 1924, was in itself provisional but sought to reduce the political dangers inherent in the reparations issue by ensuring that Germany's future payments were of a scale which would neither prevent the balancing of the German budget nor lead to inflation. A moderate scale of payments was fixed, rising in five years from £50 million to a standard rate of £125 million, and a loan of 800 million gold marks was raised, mainly in America, to help finance German payments.

It is now well known that the Dawes Plan sounded the signal for a period of recovery the scope and intensity of which were unparalleled in recent German history. This appeared to vindicate the defenders of the harsh economic treatment of the Weimar Republic at Versailles, particularly since much German capital was involved in the ensuing economic upsurge. It must be remembered, however, that this recovery owed a great deal to the large amount of foreign aid flowing into Germany between 1924 and 1929, attracted by the prospects for investment in a country whose economic development was also carefully watched over by Allied representatives carrying out the Dawes Plan. If cynics pointed out later that between 1924 and 1930 some 25.5 billion marks flowed into Germany in the form of loans and investment whereas Germany paid, ultimately, a total of some 22.9 billion marks in reparations [153], nationalist opponents of 'fulfilment' warned of the massive and dangerous debts being incurred and bitterly attacked the Allied controls [141].

Nor were German governments able to ensure that the recovery benefited all sections of German society and thereby remove the dangerous political discontent that accompanied economic hardships. It is true that governmental interference in the running of the economy increased during and after the war, as could be seen by the setting up of the *Reichsbank*, for example, or the nationalisation of the *Reichsbahn* (railway) in 1919 [148], but the failure of the revolutionary leaders to exploit their chances after 9 November 1918 put an end to plans for sweeping measures of socialisation [135]. The constitution spoke merely of the permissible step of socialising suitable private industries. The idea of 'autonomous authorities' which included representatives of appropriate sectors of society and which were to carry out nationalisation of coal, potash and steel, for example, in fact came to little in view of the vagueness of the constitutional references. The factory councils, which according to a law of 4 February 1920 were to play a central part in the running of enterprises of over twenty workers, were disappointing. If they helped in pacifying feelings they were effectively controlled by the unions and thus part of the wider clash of interests between employer and employee. The direction of all economic enterprise remained therefore the 'exclusive right of the entrepreneurs' [23 p. 556].

Employers were bound to gain some advantage from the economic expansion after 1924, for by 1929 industrial production had sur-passed the pre-war level. Of note was the increase in the number of large concerns or 'cartels', of which there were over 2,000 in Germany by 1930, in spite of anti-cartel legislation by the govern-ment in November 1923 [145]. Yet the shock of 1923 left a lasting horror. If industrialists like Stinnes had been able to profit for a time from the inflation to pay off massive debts in worthless currency, the working masses and salaried employees, functionaries of one sort or another as well as those who had lent money at fixed interest, had all been hit hard. The general effect was to transfer wealth from the thrifty, cautious sections of the lower middle class to industrialists and financiers. In addition, high unemployment levels in the later 1920s marred the 'prosperous' Germany and could not be wholly compensated for by the general rise in workers' earnings [154]. The latter were, of course, adversely affected by rising prices [139].

The situation in agriculture gave little cause for satisfaction either. German agriculture had, of course, suffered from the exhausting effort to supply Germany's wartime needs in the face of the Allied blockade, which was reflected in the low crop yields of 1920 and diminished numbers of livestock. The situation of the small farmer was made more intolerable by the absence of the sort of sweeping land reform that was the rule in eastern Europe after 1919. Some 20 per cent of cultivated soil in Germany belonged to 0.7 per cent of proprietors. The *Reichssiedlungsgesetz* (Reich Settlement Law) of 29 January 1919 foresaw the possibility of expropriating estates over 100 hectares to facilitate settlement, but it proved impossible to overcome the resistance of the landlords, and in particular of the powerful Junker aristocracy east of the Elbe, which was represented by the DNVP. Thus, between 1919 and 1928, only just over 500,000 hectares were freed by the Settlement Law, benefiting a mere 2.4 'per cent of the German farming population. The losses of 1923 compelled small farmers to borrow at exorbitant rates thereafter. Finally, agricultural prices rose more slowly than those for industrial products, of which the farms were consumers, and profits from the excellent harvests of 1928 and 1929 were offset to some extent by the high world prices. Whilst the Nazis were the hope of the white-collar urban workers, it is not surprising that rural support also became increasingly important to Hitler's movement [179; 209]. Economic pressures in Weimar Germany also go far towards explaining the difficulties in forming coalitions (Chapter 3) as well as the growing appeal of extremist parties (Chapters 6 and 7).

In general, it now appears likely that the Weimar Republic lived beyond its means. It proved impossible to expand production and foreign trade sufficiently to meet the growing costs of social welfare, unemployment relief and rising wage demands [145; 147]. However, few people think rationally about cause and effect in economic crises. What has happened to them, they feel, must be the fault of somebody, invariably the government. Truly stable societies can weather such storms, but grave difficulties were bound to arise in Weimar Germany when the economic crisis of 1929 interacted with a political and social crisis, during which vociferous opponents of democratic government could coin potent slogans and capitalise on the growing resentment against the Republican leaders.

6 LEFTIST OPPOSITION

The continuous pressure from the left and right of the political spectrum made working compromise in government infinitely more difficult to attain. During the Republic's lifetime the German Communist Party (KPD) and the Nazis (*National-Sozialistische Deutsche Arbeiterpartei* – NSDAP) were always in opposition. It was, moreover, a destructive opposition in that both movements were essentially anti-parliamentarian, although both contested elections – the KPD from 1920 onwards, the NSDAP after 1923. Furthermore, both movements generated harmful ill-feelings by being violently opposed to each other [*Doc. 23*]. Since one important element in the ultimate success of the NSDAP was its constant exploitation of the communist threat [*Doc. 16*], the problems and development of the KPD are of great interest to any historian of the Weimar Republic. That the KPD would be anti-Republican was, of course, apparent from its efforts to wrestle control of the German revolution from the SPD leaders; that the impetus towards founding the KPD was primarily intellectual – for the voting in the workers' and soldiers' councils had shown the lack of a mass following for communism (Chapter 1) – ensured that the party debate about how best to combat the new Republic was vitriolic. These internal divisions, echoing the long-standing tensions within the German Social Democratic movement as a whole, marked even the founding congress of the party between 28 December 1918 and 1 January 1919 [165].

The new party formed during these days joined the Spartacists to the so-called Left Radicals, who were centred on Bremen and had branches in North Germany, Saxony and the Rhineland. The USPD, whose leaders, for all their differences with Ebert and his colleagues, still temporised on the questions concerning Germany's future development, were excluded from the party. This break, in itself, revealed the tremendous pressures which Rosa Luxemburg had to deal with inside the KPD [160]. Although she remained deeply interested in the example of the Bolshevik seizure of power in

Russia, as was evident in the programme she drafted for the KPD early in 1919, it is by no means certain that her plans for restructuring German society would have led to the sort of terror which had marked the revolution in Russia. Whilst certainly authoritarian in her approach, she postulated a prolonged and necessary period for the education of the German masses [162]. This meant in the first instance avoiding precipitate action and contesting elections to the National Assembly in order to reach a wider audience, even though she acknowledged with Paul Levi that the National Assembly was 'the banner of counter-revolution' [43 *p. 212;* 169]. Sixty-two delegates against twenty-three voted to boycott the coming elections, and Luxemburg's subsequent death can be seen as a consequence of the failure to hold in check those members who were still intoxicated with the Russian victories of 1917 and who, in spite of the evidence, felt they could be imitated in Germany.

Looking back, 1925 appears as the turning point in the history of the KPD, when Soviet Russian influence on it became paramount. However, from 1919 until 1925 the party followed its zigzag course between those who, like the new leader from 1919–21, Paul Levi, sought to continue Luxemburg's effort to overcome the KPD's isolation in German politics and to broaden its base, and the 'leftists', who still refused to abandon the 'putschist' tactics that had cost them so dear in 1919. The failure of the KPD to play any significant role in the high point of working-class solidarity – the demonstrations that helped to put an end to Kapp's effort in 1920 (Chapter 7) – reinforced Levi's arguments. At least the party contested the elections to the first Reichstag, and by April 1920 the ultra leftists had been forced out and had organised themselves into the *Kommunistische Arbeiter Partei Deutschlands* (KAPD), which rapidly thereafter lost political influence. Yet it was Russian backing that made the then weak and ineffectual KPD into an important force. At the Halle Congress of the USPD in October 1920 the party split on the issue of whether or not to join the Third International or Comintern, the Russian-sponsored organisation designed to keep foreign communist parties in line with Moscow's policy and interests. Under the pressure of Zinoviev, the Russian president of the Comintern, who spoke at Halle, 296 delegates voted to join it against 156. Thus, by December 1920 more than half the USPD members had joined the KPD [166; 168]. For the first time it became a mass party, with almost 400,000 members, thirty-three daily newspapers and strong positions in the trade unions [131].

Levi was concerned, however, to prevent the KPD from being

dominated by the Comintern and was therefore bound to earn the animosity of Moscow, thereby stimulating the continuing efforts of the leftist members of the party. The KPD's central organisation, or *Zentrale*, was situated in Berlin, where the important leftist leaders like Ruth Fischer, Ernst Reuter and Arkadi Maslow wielded most influence. After Paul Levi's resignation from the chairmanship of the *Zentrale* in January 1921, along with his supporters, his successor, Heinrich Brandler, was both less able and less willing to counter leftist pressures for direct action. These inevitably deepened the jubilant mood created by the realisation that the KPD had become a mass party. At the same time, the Comintern emissary, the former Hungarian dictator Bela Kun, arrived in Germany to urge direct action by the KPD to alleviate Russia's current difficulties. The Bolsheviks were then in the process of negotiating the Treaty of Riga with the victorious Polish state. The outcome of such pressures was the 'March Action' of 1921 in Central Germany, where the communists hoped to exploit the internal crisis occasioned by the Allied occupation of the three Rhine ports (Chapter 5). The result was another fiasco and the rapid suppression by *Reichswehr* and police of the revolt in Saxony. Quite decisive in the failure of the KPD effort in March was the absence of widespread public support. Public opinion at large remained bitterly hostile and membership of the KPD fell to just over 180,000. Levi's subsequent open disavowal of the *Zentrale* action in March led to his expulsion, along with other 'rightist' sympathisers, from the KPD [167].

Ironically, putschist policies no longer suited Lenin, who had acknowledged after the Polish-Soviet war that the spread of communist revolution was by no means inevitable in the immediate future. Meanwhile, in the interests of attracting foreign aid and consolidating the revolution in Russia, Lenin had introduced his New Economic Policy (Chapter 4). The Third Comintern Congress in Moscow, in late June–July 1921, therefore provided the obvious occasion to discuss the failure of the March action and to effect a new Comintern line. In accordance with this, it became the policy of the new leadership of the *Zentrale* of the KPD, under Ernst Meyer, to forgo direct action. Instead, it aimed for a united front of German labour, whilst pressing simultaneously for drastic measures of socialisation. The new 'rightist' policy was not modified in 1923, underlining once more the ineptness of the KPD's tactics. In the year of the Republic's most severe crisis, little was done by the German communists beyond participating in the Social Democratic governments in Saxony and Thuringia [17; 19].

Hasty military preparations were belatedly made in October, under renewed Comintern pressure, but by this time the crisis was almost under control. The *Reichswehr* easily deposed the governments of Thuringia and Saxony, and the KPD, in the obvious absence of mass support, could achieve nothing, thus suffering a 'relatively bloodless but ultimately most decisive defeat' ['The bolshevisation of the Communist Party', *Times Literary Supplement* 25 June, 1970, pp. 685–6]. Within months, Russian control of the KPD was to become even tighter. Following Lenin's death on 21 January 1924, the triumvirate of Stalin, Kamenev and Zinoviev were struggling to establish their control in Russia against Trotsky, and it became more important to secure the unconditional support of non-Russian communist parties. In practice, this meant tightening the Bolsheviks' control over the leaders of foreign parties, which led logically to the appointment of Ernst Thälmann as leader of the KPD from 1925, a man who was prepared to be submissive to the Russians and to Stalin.

The KPD ended its *Kampfzeit* (time of struggle) and assumed its definitive form at a time when the Weimar Republic was stabilising itself internally and externally. The party's declared policy of 'concentration of forces' implied both awaiting a future struggle and yet, whilst proclaiming itself not reconciled to the Republic, continuing to contest elections with some success and playing an opposition role in the Reichstag, as well as working inside the trade unions [165]. The old problem remained: this necessary concern with 'practical politics' in a period of relative stability failed to gain for the KPD a mass following on a scale that would make revolution a feasible proposition in Germany. The ill-conceived struggle to seize power by force between 1919 and 1923 had merely isolated the KPD from the majority of the working masses, at least those in employment, for whom the traditional effort to alleviate conditions by bargaining had infinitely more appeal. Broad sectors of working-class society were in any case alienated by the excessive control exercised by the Comintern over the KPD. Right up to its downfall in 1933 the KPD failed to win over a clear majority of the German industrial workers in spite of rapid gains during the crisis, and the trade unions remained bulwarks of reformism [3; 119]. The efforts of the KPD widened the gap between itself and the SPD and thus lessened the chances of effective political resistance against the Nazis after 1929, as has so often been pointed out [Docs 12a, b]. In any case, the 'bolshevisation' of the KPD after 1923 brought with it a tightening up of the whole party structure. This left little room for the sort of flexible tactics necessary to reunite the working-class movement in Germany and tolerated only the type of leader who would submit to the bureaucratisation of the party.

There is little doubt that, unable to control the working-class movement in Weimar Germany, the KPD's tactics weakened it. The KPD can hardly, in itself, be blamed for the original defects in the SPD leadership, but its activities further inflamed moderate party, as well as nationalist, opinion against the socialist movement as a whole. This further reduced the freedom of movement of the SPD, so fateful after 1929. In that sense, the KPD's development reflected the obsessively selfish concern of other Weimar parties with sectional interests. Ironically, when the KPD appeared to be more of a serious threat during its *Kampfzeit*, conservative and anti-republican groups in the Reichstag were arguably less inclined to push their opposition to government policies to extremes. Such restraint was less apparent after 1923, when the KPD's day-to-day activities possessed simply a potential nuisance value, although this, of course, changed after 1930 (Chapter 9). In that respect at least, the reduced KPD threat during the years of relative stability might even have weakened the basis of democracy in the Republic [5; 161]. Either way, for many historians, it appears that the KPD could do no right.

Perhaps it is indeed time for the more redeeming features of the KPD to be examined. The passionate devotion to the party's ideals by its supporters – suffering as they often were from economic hardship and unemployment – helped to offset the bureaucratic rigidity of the KPD's organisation. Its membership fluctuated wildly and bore a relationship with the current economic and political development of Germany but one of its strengths, as was pointed out by a German observer in 1932, was precisely its trenchant criticism of the German economic and political system [131]. Preparation for more forceful opposition had not, of course, ceased after the failures of 1923, and one must note finally the significance of the KPD's paramilitary force, the *Rote Frontkämpferbund*, formed by Thälmann in 1924. Unlike the other similar force formed to fight the opponents of the Republic in 1924, the *Reichsbanner Schwarz-Rot-Gold*, which rapidly developed into an arm of the SPD, the KPD's fighters were later able to play a more important role in the defence of the working classes against the Nazi street gangs. With its two associated groups, the *Rote Jungfront* and *Rote Marine*, the *Rote Frontkämpferbund* had already reached a membership of some 100,000 in 1924. Moreover, the KPD energetically combated the penetration of working-class locales and meeting places by national-socialist activists [170].

7 RIGHTIST OPPOSITION

In considering right-wing opposition to the Weimar Republic one is immediately struck by its depth, range and variety, as well as by the force of its ideological traditions. At one level was the antipathy of the powerful conservative forces of Wilhelmine Germany, whom the revolution had failed to break, manifesting itself in the DNVP, in the *Reichswehr* (Chapter 8) and in the authoritarian civil service, bureaucracy and judiciary, not to mention the Church. The anti-Republican sentiments of these authorities could result in a less than impartial repression of communist or left-wing activities and a markedly more lenient treatment of the *Freikorps* leaders or even of Hitler in 1923. This was furthermore a bureaucracy, the function of which was all the more important in view of its continuous day-to-day activities during the turbulent periods of party political struggle [42]. At another level was the hostility of the numerous *Freikorps* and paramilitary groups thriving in early post-war Germany. These rejected the return to organised life and unemployment, but were also called on at key moments to support the Republic. Finally, there were the numerous *völkisch* groups which had their roots in the pre-war period and which the National Socialist German Workers' Party (NSDAP) came to dominate [175; 202].

The difficulty of drawing strict lines between the segments of the rightist opposition can be shown by referring briefly to the values implicit in the term *völkisch*, the stress on German race and purity, the exaltation of specifically German characteristics and the pronounced anti-Semitism. They were shared to a greater or lesser extent throughout the right, the more so on account of the general radicalisation of right-wing thought resulting from the bitter experiences of the First World War and defeat. The existence of a powerful, potentially explosive mixture of discontent, resentment and sheer frustration on the right was indisputable. At its most extreme form it was demonstrated by the three hundred or so political murders which took place in Germany between 1918 and

1922 [180] [*Doc. 14*]. How this force could be mobilised for more constructive ends was quite another matter.

The only available political party, at first, for the conservatives and nationalists was the DNVP, and its strengths and shortcomings are therefore of obvious interest. The DNVP, founded in November 1918, was the heir not only of the two former conservative parties of Wilhelmine Germany but of the Christian Socialists and of the pre-war racist and anti-semitic organisations like the Pan German League. The largely Protestant-dominated DNVP, made up as it was from a wide range of social groups, set out determinedly to build a mass following and to achieve 'the organisation of all forces that wished with a holy seriousness for the real reconstruction of our downtrodden fatherland on the basis of traditional values' [178]. At first, the DNVP was more or less held together by its negative attitude towards the Republic. In accordance with its monarchist outlook, its policy between 1919 and 1924 was one of outright opposition, relying, if anything, on the rather unrealistic hope that it might gain power, hand in hand with forceful action by the *Reichswehr* [198; 219].

By 1923, however, such a negative outlook had come to seem futile to the important economic pressure groups associated with the DNVP. Over half the party's Reichstag members belonged to the powerful organisation of landowners, the *Reichslandbund* [31], and these, for example, saw participation in government as a means of fighting for the reinstatement of agrarian tariffs. The smaller industrial representation in the DNVP was interested, on the other hand, in the economic prospects offered by the Dawes Plan [188]. Such broader considerations argued in favour of responding to DVP overtures for the DNVP to take part in government (Chapter 3). Moreover, the various right-wing efforts to seize power or overturn the government – Kapp in 1920, Hitler in 1923 – had been suppressed, and the head of the *Reichswehr*, Seeckt, had made no decisive move to seize the reins of government during the crisis. The DNVP leadership under Count Cuno Westarp was thus bound to respond to the pressure of many DNVP supporters for the party to shoulder some of the burdens of governing Germany and to work from inside to change a state which was abhorrent to them. At the same time, the die-hard sectors of the party, whose spokesman rapidly became Alfred Hugenberg, continued to urge all-out opposition [198].

In 1924, the internally weak state of the party was made plainer when fifty-two of its Reichstag deputies voted in favour of the

Dawes Plan and forty-eight against. The 'realists' had their way when the DNVP participated in first the Luther then the Marx cabinets. Such promising trends towards the DNVP being assimilated in the party system of the Republic never fully developed, however, owing to the persistent reaction from the extreme right wing of the party and its associated extra-parliamentary groups. Their views seemed vindicated by the fact that the mere presence of the DNVP in Weimar governments did not bring about either the desired economic benefits (Chapter 3) or a reversal of Stresemann's foreign policy. Thus Westarp's situation became an acutely difficult one, whatever his own personal defects in leading the party. Since the electoral reverses of 1928 were interpreted by the right of the DNVP as the outcome of collaborating with the detested middle parties, the way was open for Hugenberg to become First Party Chairman. In contrast to Westarp, he had little taste for compromise and opted decisively in favour of retaining the support and good will of the more rampant nationalists. Hugenberg, who brought his money and powerful press to his cause, wrote in 1928: 'I believe in a government by the elect few, not by the elected. ... I believe in leaders, not in speakers. Words are enemies of action. ... I believe in government by strong men who have the will power and the strength to carry out national decisions' [178]. None the less, Hugenberg's espousal of the *Führerprinzip* was bound to lose him, in time, the support of the more moderate sections of the DNVP, although it was a direct result of the party's wider failure to reconcile the pressures from its extreme supporters with the dictates of office. That, after all, demanded give and take with the other responsible Weimar parties.

The NSDAP, which had been founded in 1919 and which Hitler rapidly came to dominate, naturally did not have this particular problem. It remained doggedly in opposition until Hitler came in not just as a member of a coalition, but to play the central role in government. There are more than enough accounts of Hitler's rise and eventual arrival in high office in 1933 to make a chronological description of these events superfluous in a study which is primarily an analysis of some of the problems of the Weimar Republic. An obvious starting point is to consider the effects of Hitler's abortive 'march on Berlin' in 1923. The fiasco of that year reinforced Hitler's conviction that the NSDAP had to work harder to become a truly mass movement. This required it to devote itself systematically to electoral activities and commit itself to following the 'legal' road to winning over a majority of voters [179]. It is useful to stress that for seven years these tactics brought virtually no return in terms of significantly measurable increases in electoral support, the NSDAP gaining a mere 2.6 per cent of the votes cast in the 1928 elections [186]. What is significant, however, is the way in which, during that period, Hitler further clarified the priorities of his movement and refined and extended the organisational bureaucracy of his party. This laborious process goes far to explain how he was able to profit from the successful electoral breakthrough of the movement when it came in due course [194]. It goes without saying that the very effort to fight electoral campaigns required a streamlining of the party's organisation. Here it is possible to see a clear connection between the nature of the support Hitler sought to attract and the distinctive organisational form of the NSDAP, with its emphasis on the all-seeing, all-powerful Führer [172; 195].

That can best be understood by stressing, firstly, that the NSDAP was built up not only on protest but on resentment. This is evident from its 'programmatic' utterances, as well as the character and background of the party's chief followers and leading officials. Hitler, of course, incorporated in his own person many of the major features on which his movement thrived: the deep sense of frustration; the hate against Jews and Marxists, whom Hitler repeatedly insisted were one and the same thing; the dislike of parliamentary democracy; and the profound dissatisfaction with his own position in society [205]. To build up a genuinely mass movement from such beginnings, and to keep it together, required unique personal qualities. It was clear, for example, from the very beginning that the NSDAP depended heavily on Hitler's spectacular public-speaking skills. At the forty-six NSDAP gatherings held between November 1919 and November 1920, Hitler appeared on no fewer than thirty-one occasions as the star speaker [172]. An interesting circular process soon became apparent. The greater the range and variety of supporters attracted to Hitler, and the more potent his appeals became for refuting the existing order, the more crucial became his own personal status as the sole leader capable of holding together such diverse elements. In turn, the dynamism of the movement and its fanaticism and rejection of any compromise justified his growing insistence, particularly after his emergence from prison and the party's re-founding early in 1925, on his unconditional authority as the Führer at the apex of a strictly hierarchical party structure [208].

This position was essential for him to exercise the power necessary to adapt the party's tactics to the exigencies of the movement and thus, like some mathematical progression, to extend still further the appeal of the NSDAP. As early as 1921 Hitler was indeed able to force through within the party leadership circles his views on the uniqueness of the NSDAP amidst the welter of post-war *völkisch* groups. So successful was he in insisting on this that the growth of the still small, not to say insignificant NSDAP, from 27,000 in 1925 to 108,000 in 1928, resulted chiefly from its absorption of most of Germany's racist and *völkisch* groups, as well as followers from the very young and from such *Freikorps* units as *Oberland* and *Wiking* [175]. Ultimately, of course, Hitler required the sort of organisation that could control more than the extremists on the right. It was therefore of the greatest importance that he convinced his fellow party leaders to accept his newer, omnipotent image after 1925. Whilst attempting to become a mass movement, the NSDAP remained essentially anti-parliamentarian and therefore, at its inner core at least, a conspiratorial movement [*Doc. 15*]. Hence the importance of Hitler's choice of fellow conspirators, who would in time be able to manipulate a mass following under his direction.

The centre of the movement for Hitler's purposes had to be Bavaria, a base which had already provided him with important contacts with higher officialdom prior to 1925 and where, in the atmosphere engendered by memories of the 'red revolution' of 1919, his appeal was very obvious [172]. It was vital that other groups, formed outside Bavaria, should accept the commands from party headquarters in Munich. Yet, given the fact that Hitler was forbidden to speak publicly in much of Germany after 1923, the growth of the NSDAP was greatly dependent on the initiatives of local and regional party and *Sturmabteiling* (SA) leaders. In the conditions of hardship and struggle during the lean years between 1925 and 1930, Hitler needed supporters who had the ability to command local followings and the toughness to hold their own against rivals [181; 182; 206]. An analysis of the *Gauführer* of the NSDAP shows older men, mostly grown up before 1914, with extensive but generally incomplete educational backgrounds, not from a purely proletarian milieu and with a record of having either fought for a period in post-war *Freikorps* or border defence units. They had often failed in an effort to return to professional life [172]. Clearly, such men as Gregor Strasser, the party's leader in North Germany, or Julius Streicher in Nuremberg, who made up the 'old fighters' of the early NSDAP movement, were never entirely disposed to accept the structure of command which promised in due course to elevate Hitler to the level of an almost mythical figure, high above the party bureaucracy and routines but with the right to interfere anywhere and at any time in the functioning of that machine [197; 208]. Hitler's ability to surmount their criticism, largely because they accepted in the final resort the arguments in favour of his personal power in the movement, could never entirely eliminate lingering resentments. This applied even more to the SA, originally founded in August 1921 as the party's paramilitary body to keep order at meetings and to make party propaganda. The SA was reorganised in 1925 and began wearing its brown uniform in the same year. The replacement of its original leader, Ernst Röhm, by Franz Pfeffer von Salomon in 1926 reflected Hitler's determination to confine the SA to supporting the political organisation and to inhibit it from behaving like other *Freikorps* units, as a revolutionary and often almost autonomous fighting force. Again, Hitler was never entirely successful in suppressing the revolutionary mood in the ranks of the SA, which became more troublesome after 1930 [184].

Notwithstanding these problems, Hitler's authority over his party offered a staggering contrast with that of other party leaders of the Republic, with the notable exception of the KPD. The KPD, however, based itself on the class struggle, whereas the NSDAP appeared in fact to transcend classes. This, paradoxically, derived from the flexibility of movement which Hitler achieved with his control of the party machinery. It enabled him to widen continually the scope of his propaganda and appeal. Partly because of this, the truly revolutionary nature of the NSDAP was often not fully apparent to many of Hitler's contemporaries. The party's original programme was presented early in 1920. Its twenty-five points displayed the movement's nationalist credentials for all to see, in its rejection of the peace treaties, in its call for the union of all Germans in a 'Greater Germany', in its racist stress on 'German blood' as the test for membership of the German state and thus its rejection of all Jews. Its 'socialist' pedigree was vaunted in its concern for the state to promote the individual's work and welfare, in its demand for profit-sharing in the 'great industries', in its call for the nationalisation of large businesses and in its references to land reform, in the interests of the community as a whole [207]. Such anti-capitalist sentiments were considerably played down later on, in the years before the seizure of power. Hitler often, in his early speeches, spoke proudly of his originality in coupling 'national' with 'socialist', and indeed the NSDAP's programme is symptomatic of the deliberate attempt to exclude no support that might be forthcoming in Germany. In 1926 the programme was declared immutable, in order to stifle internal party conflicts, on the grounds that these deflected energy from the drive towards power. A contemporary observer of the German scene remarked cynically of the programme: 'In spite of their [the terms'] decreed immutability they are neither clear nor binding for purposes of practical policy'[131 *p. 73*].

This was, in fact, only true up to a point. Policy was invariably decided by Hitler, and his tactics *were* influenced by the desire to command the maximum following. The force of his movement derived, after all, from its dynamic criticism of the existing order, its negations of the *status quo*: 'It is best to assume these negations as the solitary, definable position. With them the movement became great' [131 *pp. 73–4; 179*]. Nonetheless, the party had no hesitation in associating itself openly with policies harmful to democracy during its campaigning. Thus, the disturbing emphasis on anti-Semitism remained pronounced, as did the stress on the communist menace; the scarcely veiled contempt for party politics and parliamentary democracy continued [*Doc. 17*], as did the violent denunciation of Germany's external enemies [191]. This core of ideas did not, of course, preclude adjustments in the party's electoral thrust if this meant an increase in its membership and following. One obvious example is the party's targeting of the rural vote from around 1928.

Hitler had originally hoped to win mass support from the working classes by drawing an attractive picture of their place in the future *völkisch* state towards which the movement was working. 'What we want is not a state of drones but a state which gives to everyone that to which on the basis of his own activity he has a right' [131 *p. 73*]. Concentration on winning over the urban masses could also be reconciled with the Nazi denunciations of democracy, since massive Nazi support in the towns might presumably have produced the sort of revolutionary movement whose sheer weight, as was the case in November 1918, would have crushed the existing order, leaving the way free for the mass party to rule. However, although the NSDAP *did* make inroads into the working-class vote [186; 195; 204], the party never secured the following it wanted from most German workers, who remained loyal on the whole before 1933 to the SPD and KPD. Hence the importance of Hitler's 'rural-nationalist' plan, to exploit the growing discontent among the small farmers of the countryside (Chapter 5). His control of the party was again clearly demonstrated, for this change of emphasis meant in effect restructuring the entire organization of the NSDAP. The territorial units (*Gau*) into which the party was organised were redrawn, so that they now coincided roughly with the boundaries of Reichstag electoral districts. This decisive demonstration of Hitler's capacity to act as both leader and programmer was followed by 'clarification' of point 17 of the party programme of 1920. It was now explained that 'expropriation of land for com- munal purposes with compensation' did not mean that the NSDAP was against private property as such; rather, the clause referred merely to property illegally acquired or not used in accordance with community interests, that is by 'mainly Jewish speculators' [207].

In sum, the NSDAP showed a remarkable capacity to be flexible in its wooing of the German electorate, making steady inroads in established parties and slowly building up a national-socialist constituency. The party's appeal transcended class lines, although middle-class voters continued to give it most support. The massive surge of support for the NSDAP in 1930 was primarily rooted in the 'panic' of the German middle classes [3] and their conviction during the economic crisis that the established political parties would not save them from ruin. If there were long-standing 'traits' of German historical and intellectual developments which predisposed certain sectors of German society towards the NSDAP, this brief analysis of the party confirms how important it is also to give full weight to the general crisis in Germany after 1929. Only then did Hitler's gamble begin to pay off; and it was a gamble, not only because the world economic crisis could hardly have been predicted. There was also a risk that, in focusing the movement's energy so aggressively on acquiring power, it would be more difficult to control the rank and file unless power was achieved quickly. Finally, the NSDAP's remarkable ability to widen its appeal must not be allowed to obscure the remarkable consistency of ideas and long-term aims of Hitler and his fellow party leaders [191]. The implications of this, unfortunately, were rather more clear after 1933 than before.

8 *REICHSWEHR* AND POLITICS

Ebert's unwillingness to sanction far-reaching revolutionary changes and his desire to prepare for elections had led him to rely on the old German army to keep order. Its officers complied, thereby saving their own skins and strengthening their foothold in the new Republic by helping Ebert to crush his political enemies on the extreme left [*Doc. 18a*]. That this process was not easy to reverse was confirmed by the law of March 1919 on the provisional *Reichswehr* (as the new German army was called). Although this specifically referred to the army being formed on a 'democratic basis', it was difficult to see how this could be realised, in so far as the law in effect sanctioned the *status quo* by permitting the recently formed *Freikorps* to form the basis of the *Reichswehr*, under the control of the old officers [225]. Essentially anti-Republican forces thus formed the core of the new army. Its structure was further determined by the military provisions of the Treaty of Versailles, which eventually became law in Germany once the treaty was accepted. According to the treaty, the army was to be composed of seven infantry and three cavalry divisions under no more than two army corps headquarters. The army was not to exceed 100,000 men, serving for twelve years, although up to 4,000 officers were permitted to enlist for twenty-five years. No more than 5 per cent of the effective forces were to be replaced each year. The army was to possess no offensive weapons, no aeroplanes, no tanks, and other arms allowed to Germany were listed in detail. The celebrated Great General Staff was to be abolished, as were the military academies and cadet schools. All measures of mobilisation or preparation for mobilisation were forbidden, as was the manufacture or import of poison gas and other war materials. Any weapons surplus to those permitted by the Allies had to be handed over in due course. Similar detailed provisions were made for the German navy, including the express forbidding of submarine manufacture [223; 225].

These measures clearly revealed the Allied distrust of German 'militarism' and of the powerful traditions of the old German officer corps. The German army – the first unified army in Germany's history, since the once separate contingents and military authorities of the separate states no longer existed under the new constitution – was thus clearly to be restricted to a virtual 'police' force. It was strong enough to keep internal order but not to wage another war. Not the least important implication of the Versailles military terms, however, was that they made it even more unlikely that the *Reichswehr* would undergo future 'democratic' reforms. The emphasis on a small professional army – a reflection of the Allied fears about the former mass levies of pre-war Germany – attracted the rightist *Freikorps* mentality rather than the republican moderates, for want of a better term. The fact that Germany was to be allowed only a small army seemed to argue in favour of leaving it in the hands of those who knew best how to make the most of it – namely, the officers of pre-war Germany.

Uneasy relationships between the *Reichswehr* and the Republic were almost certain, for the world of the officer corps had been that of personal allegiance to the Kaiser and a highly privileged position in German society [226; 228]. The Republic was hardly 'doomed at birth' because of its early reliance on the army, since much depended on personalities and on future developments. Some of the immediate post-war conflicts, however, gave warning of the problems involved. There were few officers – though some did exist – who shared the readiness of Walther Reinhardt, the first Chief of the Army Command, to co-operate closely with the Republic. With such a man, Gustav Noske, the Minister of Defence, might have had some hope of integrating the *Reichswehr* into the Republic, but in 1919 Reinhardt became increasingly isolated not only from his fellow officers but from the *Freikorps* leaders, who continued to nurse the hope of direct action against the Republic [225]. The resentment of the *Freikorps* formations, many of whom faced unemployment on returning to civilian life, was an important factor in the so-called Kapp Putsch in 1920 [229].

After the commander of the *Reichswehr* district which included Berlin, General von Lüttwitz, refused to disband the radical Erhardt brigade, this particular *Freikorps* formation marched into the city on the night of 12–13 March. The cabinet was forced to leave Berlin and a 'government' was set up under Lüttwitz and Wolfgang Kapp, a former Prussian civil servant. In point of fact, Kapp was, in time, isolated not only by a universally hostile public opinion and by the general strike called against him, but by the response of the key *Reichswehr* leaders. Admittedly, Reinhardt was virtually alone in wanting the *Reichswehr* to put down the rebels, but whilst the attitude of the other officers towards the coup was ambiguous to say the least, and certainly not positively in favour of the Republic, in the last resort they placed the unity of the army above Kapp, whose action threatened to split it beyond repair. Deprived of effective support, Kapp eventually fled the country and Bauer's government was able to return to the capital [225; 234].

Whilst the Putsch showed the futility of frontal attacks on the Republic, Noske's efforts to integrate the *Reichswehr* into the Republic were discredited, and the gap between SPD and army leaders widened. How imprisoned the SPD leaders none the less remained within their conceptual framework was shown by their reluctance to exploit divisions in the *Reichswehr*. Instead, they followed with devastating logic the consequences of their original reliance on the old army leaders and replaced Reinhardt – 'the one General who was prepared to defend the Republic by force of arms' [225 *p. 103*] – with a man whom they believed would have the confidence of the officers and men, General Hans von Seeckt. Seeckt's activity as Chief of the Army Command between 1920 and 1926 gave the *Reichswehr* its definitive structure. In 1919 Seeckt had been head of the so-called *Truppenamt*, which in effect exercised the functions of the now forbidden General Staff. Like Reinhardt, Seeckt accepted the need for co-operation between *Reichswehr* and Republic but had no interest in bringing about real integration.

It would be more accurate to say the *Reichswehr* was prepared to tolerate the Republic for the time being in its own interests. *Reichswehr* and government became, as it were, coalition partners, both sharing a concern for stable political developments, since civil war threatened the unity of the state as well as that of the army. As Seeckt had, in effect, urged in response to suggestions to use force against Kapp, '*Reichswehr* does not fire on *Reichswehr*'. Such internal conflicts had to be avoided at all costs in the interest of concentrating on the long-term objectives of restoring Germany's greatness and preparing for a future struggle against the Versailles powers [227]. It seemed to Seeckt that the spirit of discipline, unity and obedience of the old German army could best be fostered in the *Reichswehr* by building a 'Chinese wall' around it to protect it as far as possible from outside influences [225; 237]. In effect, this meant that only the supreme leaders of the *Reichswehr* could concern themselves with politics. That was the real meaning of the 'non-political' *Reichswehr* and it demanded, in a time of excessive interest in politics, that the mass of the troops be politically neutral and simply obedient [*Doc. 18b*]. The impact of Seeckt's work and ideas on the *Reichswehr* will be understood by looking at its structure of command and its composition, as well as by examining its attitude to important political events.

A prerequisite for Seeckt's policies was to secure for the Chief of the Army Command the necessary power and authority, since neither the Versailles Peace, nor the German constitution nor the law on the army (*Wehrgesetz*) of 23 March 1921 provided for the sort of supreme military leader that Seeckt had in mind. The key lay with the Minister of Defence, who was permitted to exercise the supreme command over the Reich's military forces by the Reich President, in whom the command was vested. The fact was that Seeckt's personal ascendancy over the Defence Minister who succeeded Noske, the Democrat Otto Gessler, produced a reversal of the roles originally allotted to the Chief of Army Command and Defence Minister. In practice, Seeckt took all important military and political decisions in the Ministry of Defence and thus, although not himself answerable to the Reichstag, gained access to cabinet meetings and to the President, whilst Gessler was more or less reduced to covering up for the *Reichswehr* in the Reichstag and in public as the 'responsible' minister. It is true that, after Seeckt's resignation, Gessler tried to redress the balance by taking advantage of the lesser personality of Seeckt's successor, General Heye. Gessler then had to reckon, however, with the growing importance of his own nominee in the new Wehrmacht Department, Kurt von Schleicher. The latter had already gained his experience under Seeckt. Groener's arrival at the Defence Ministry in 1928 naturally reduced the importance of Heye, but Groener also relied heavily on Schleicher who, as the head of the new *Ministeramt* in the Defence Ministry from 1929, exercised the political influence which Seeckt alone had been able to combine with military powers. The latter were wielded by Heye's successor in 1930, General Kurt Freiherr von Hammerstein-Equord, a man who had close personal links with Groener and Schleicher going back over many years. In short, the influence Seeckt had secured for the military in his own person remained in the trinity of Schleicher, Groener and Hammerstein. The close links persisted between the top *Reichswehr* leaders and the President [*Doc. 21*] and minimised, as Seeckt had desired, the area of contact between *Reichswehr* and Republican institutions [225; 227].

The alienation between *Reichswehr* and Republic can, of course, also be seen by examining the composition of the army, which was in turn affected by the *Freikorps* formations of post-war Germany. The political outlook of these was rightist, composed as they were of professional officers and NCOs of the imperial army, and their resentment against the Republic made them thoroughly disruptive factors in post-war Germany. The sympathies of most of the *Reichswehr* leaders also lay with the right in German politics, but the success of Seeckt's policies depended on avoiding a repetition of the Kapp Putsch, which might provoke premature action and a split in the *Reichswehr*. Nor did the emphasis of the Officer Corps on discipline and tradition have room for the extremism of the *Freikorps* formations and of the group loyalty of these to their own leaders [*Doc. 14*]. On the other hand, the *Reichswehr* had been based on the *Freikorps* formations and it was precisely from such circles that the army could expect to draw most of its recruits, given the refusal of the officers to enlist men from the left. Although the *Freikorps* were dissolved after the Kapp Putsch, they continued to exist in underground or terrorist groups such as *Organisation Escherich* (*Orgesch*) or *Organisation Consul* and were partially reconstituted in 1923 [175]. Indeed, they formed an essential pool of reserves in times of crisis, for they also possessed extensive arms and equipment. An illegal 'Black Reichswehr' was one way of avoiding some of the limitations of Versailles [234]. Although at the end of 1923 Seeckt again sought to draw a clear line between the *Freikorps* formations and the regular troops, the love-hate relationship persisted.

Particularly close co-operation developed in due course between the *Reichswehr* and the largest and most important paramilitary group, the *Stahlhelm*. This relationship contrasted markedly with the coolness between the *Reichswehr* and the *Reichsbanner*, which, of course, had been set up in 1924 by the SPD deputy in the Prussian parliament, Otto Hörsing, specifically to rally Republican forces against such groups as the *Stahlhelm* [9]. Such a state of affairs was perhaps unavoidable, in view of the extraordinarily conservative disposition of the officer corps. The latter continued to rely on the traditional recruiting grounds of the old Prussian force, the sons of former officers and of the professions. It is revealing that on average 21 per cent of army officers came from the nobility, although the latter comprised a mere 0.14 per cent of the German population. Such men could be expected to continue recruiting from paramilitary circles, although the process inevitably gave rise to conflicts with civilian and particularly Prussian authorities. Even following the resignation of Seeckt, when slightly better relations existed between government and *Reichswehr*, the former, not the latter, went more than half way to legalise an illegal procedure by closer financial control of the 'black' funds. These totalled 3,380,000 marks in 1928–29 and came increasingly from public money, rather than from the private contributions of agriculture and industry on which Seeckt had relied [8].

Such dubious relationships were arguably simply the reflection of Seeckt's self-imposed task of watchdog over 'German' interests and of his constant activity in high politics. All of this made it difficult for a soundly based relationship to evolve between *Reichswehr* and state. Seeckt's own political ambitions were manifested from the very moment the Republic came into being and for some time ran parallel with those of the DNVP (Chapter 7). In 1923 he perpetually harassed and eventually secured the resignation of Gustav Stresemann, the leader of the government of the day trying to deal with the grave crisis facing Germany. Seeckt's action against leftist risings in 1923 contrasted with his delay in suppressing the Bavarian separatists in that year because that would have meant *Reichswehr* firing on *Reichswehr*. Only Hitler's unsuccessful putsch, crushed by the police, saved Seeckt from the need to act. It remains a depressing fact that his possible move against the constitution was thwarted when Ebert shrewdly placed the responsibility for defending the Republic squarely on Seeckt's shoulders by giving him emergency powers on the night of 8–9 November. 'The fiction', a German historian neatly commented, 'that the *Reichswehr* was the trustee of the state thus became a legal reality' [228 *p. 192*]. If Seeckt's prompt relinquishment of his emergency powers on 1 March 1924 – to the chagrin of the DNVP – did add to the *Reichswehr*'s standing in official circles, it is possible that Seeckt acted so in order to leave himself free to stand as President at the close of Ebert's term of office. These were all extraordinary steps to take for the leader of a state's army, as was Seeckt's irresponsible insistence on the primacy of German-Russian relations in the face of Stresemann's wider political strategy (Chapter 4) [72] [*Doc. 7c*].

Seeckt's views on the political role of the army survived his own resignation in 1926, following the uproar over the participation of the eldest son of the Crown Prince, William, in the exercises of Infantry Regiment Nine. Admittedly, the possibility of the army playing a more constructive role in the Republic came to seem less remote in the relatively stable period after Hindenburg became President in 1925, giving the *Reichswehr* a focal point in the Republic. Heye and Schleicher encouraged a degree of *rapprochement* between *Reichswehr* and Republic which was a considerable advance on Seeckt's attitude. However, their view of the nature of the army remained essentially the same as that of their predecessor. There was little sign that *rapprochement* would lead to integration in the near future. Although the activities of the *Reichswehr* came under greater public scrutiny, the SPD continued to pay the penalty of its earlier errors, and its attacks on the *Reichswehr* remained isolated incidents rather than the expression of any concerted effort to force the army towards more constructive reforms [3].

It had been clear earlier that peaceful coexistence between *Reichswehr* and Republic was not enough in itself to weather any serious crisis with safety. The events of 1923 had shown that when the interests of political and military leaders were opposed, the threat lurked of direct action by the *Reichswehr*. The risk was more acute when the officers faced demands within the army to act, again as in 1923. Those internal pressures testified to Seeckt's difficulty in keeping politics out of the *Reichswehr* ranks. Because of the social composition of the *Reichswehr*, as well as its pattern of recruitment, it was likely to be increasingly difficult to resist the attraction of the NSDAP once Hitler began to advance towards the centre of the political arena. Groener and Schleicher thus faced the dilemma of Seeckt in a particularly acute form after 1928. In the words of the Social Democrat Julius Leber in 1931:

> I fear the *Reichswehr* has been built upon a colossal mistake of von Seeckt's. He believed that discipline was enough, and obedience to the commander's will was a sufficient guarantee of the proper functioning of the Army. But no unit in these times will place itself unreservedly in the hands of its commander. The links between the soldiers and the public are too intimate for that and far too closely concerned with social and political trends of every sort [228 *p. 195*].

Thus, in spite of regulations to the contrary, national socialism penetrated the armed forces through the younger ranks and officers and there found fertile ground to exploit in the growing discontent with an 'a-political' *Reichswehr*. Such pressures towards 'action' could not be ignored indefinitely by the army leaders, as the crisis was soon to show.

One might finally ask what sort of fighting force had been built up as a result of the policy of the *Reichswehr* leaders, since the desire to prepare for a future war of liberation had been a major justification of their actions after 1918. Clearly, the refinement of the structure of authority in the Ministry of Defence after 1920, the consolidation of relations with the Russian military after 1921, the links between *Reichswehr* and the paramilitary forces on the right – all of these factors helped to build the core of a more powerful army than was necessary to fulfil the policing functions assigned to it by the Versailles terms, in spite of Allied inspection and controls [227]. Through the innocuous-sounding *Truppenamt* in the Ministry of Defence were exercised the functions of the illegal Great General Staff. Here the future army leaders of the Third Reich gained their experience. Technical developments were also made possible through the Russian connections. The German flying base operating in Lipetsk after 1924 was particularly important, for here fighter pilots were trained and valuable testing and technical innovation took place. A tank school had been opened at Kama by 1929. More systematic co-operation and training links were eventually established between the *Reichswehr* and some of the paramilitary bodies, in particular with the *Stahlhelm*, whose flying groups were used in 1932 to launch a *Wehrrflug-organisation* embracing all trained flying personnel outside the army. Yet whilst the *Reichswehr's* *potential* for expansion was considerable, at least as far as manpower was concerned, there was still a dearth of equipment. By early 1931, for example, it had only six medium and four light tanks, although plans had been drawn up to increase the number. Great advances had, of course, been made with the air force, and at the end of 1930 the decision was taken to create a secret force of aeroplanes in direct violation of Versailles. However, the gap remained between plans and achievement. In 1931 there were still only 29 reconnaissance planes, 15 fighter planes and 26 night bombers, but the number of pilots trained at Lipetsk alone in 1933 was 120, and this gives an inkling of potential developments [225].

PART THREE: CONCLUSION

9 THE CRISIS AND HITLER

Implicit in this study has been the assumption that no single problem caused the downfall of the Weimar Republic, that the interaction of these problems, many of which pre-dated the Republic, progressively weakened the new German state, and that, for specific reasons which will be examined in this conclusion, the process reached its climax in the crisis of 1929–33. In that respect, the novelty of these years is in part a question of degree. The gravity of the political crisis could already be gauged by the difficulties of Social Democrat Herman Müller, who was Chancellor between June 1928 and March 1930, in forming a cabinet which would command sufficient support in the Reichstag, notwithstanding the seemingly favourable election results of May 1928. In fact, Müller's 'Great Coalition' emerged from the device of a 'cabinet of personalities' who could hope to use any influence they had with their respective parliamentary delegations in order to get together a majority to support the government on at least vital issues, but could not bind those delegations to the government in any formal way [*Doc. 19*]. Meanwhile, the class conflict which the 1918 revolution had failed to solve, and which underlay coalition difficulties, was now aggravated by a mounting financial and economic crisis.

The force of this statement can be seen by examining briefly the internal state of those parties represented in the 'Great Coalition' – the SPD, the Democrats, the DVP, the Centre Party and the BVP. Of the Democrats, loyal supporters of the Republic, it is enough to remind ourselves of their remorseless decline which the May elections confirmed. The Catholic camp lost votes, too, at these elections, but from Müller's viewpoint the ominous sign was the replacement of Marx, who resigned the leadership of the Centre Party to Monsignor Ludwig Kaas in December 1928. Kaas's victory over rival candidates Joseph Joos and Adam Stegerwald, who were both close to the Catholic labour movement, confirmed the general swing to the right. Undoubtedly, however, the most striking illustration of the proposition that parties reflected the unresolved class conflict was the confrontation between the DVP and the SPD [3; 131]. It was obvious that by 1929 only Stresemann's personality was preventing the DVP from sliding finally to the right, whereas Müller's position was made difficult not simply by the growing pressures from the Reichstag faction of the SPD but from the trade unions and from the leftist opposition groups within the party. These grew more troublesome after 1925 and captured some 35 per cent of the votes in the debate about coalition parties and armaments at the Magdeburg Party Congress of 1929 [19; 117]. The polarisation of political principles was accentuated not so much yet by any threat from the extreme left or right (which was not acute even when Müller fell) as by its very existence during the economic crisis. In 1928, true to its subservience to Moscow, the KPD changed its tactics to complement Stalin's own internal struggle and broke off what collaboration had existed with the SPD, branding the latter as 'Social Fascists' and thereby confusing political issues and increasing Müller's difficulties [165) [*Doc. 12b*]. On the right, Hugenberg exploited his position as leader of the DNVP to organise the 'National Opposition' against the recent Young Plan, after setting up in July a committee representing his own party, the *Stahlhelm*, the Pan German League and the NSDAP [198].

This radicalisation of politics, in part pre-dating the economic crisis, significantly circumscribed Müller's freedom of action. It became more difficult to build working agreements between factions, which in turn prevented the political leadership from tackling the crisis quickly. This, in turn, helped to complete the vicious circle by intensifying inter-party disputes over the best solutions to economic problems [*Doc. 20*]. It has already been shown that the Republic's economic difficulties were never entirely overcome in the so-called 'prosperous' period. Germany's failure to develop an active trade balance, the decline in tax revenues and the increased expenditure on unemployment insurance through the Reich Institute for Unemployment Insurance, which had been set up in 1927, all combined to produce and maintain budget deficits [145; 147]. The Young Plan, which was put into its final form at the Hague Conference in August 1929, did indeed free Germany from the irksome restrictions of the Dawes Plan and paved the way for the final, if posthumous, act of Stresemann's diplomacy in the French evacuation of the Rhineland in 1930. The Young Plan contained a fifty-nine-year schedule of reparations payments amounting to 2.05 billion marks and permitting possible deferment of two-thirds of the annuities, though under stringent conditions. The fact that all German funds were in future to come from the general budget clearly indicated the expectation that Germany would continue to prosper.

None the less, once the Wall Street Crash of 1929 opened the way for the flight of capital from Germany and Europe, the reparations payments created intolerable strains on the already creaking Reich finances, not least because they appeared to render more difficult the devaluation of the German currency as a possible solution to the economic and financial crisis [26; 145].

In itself, this fact made more potent the appeal of the virulent nationalist mood orchestrated by the extreme right both against the Young Plan and indeed against co-operation in general with the Allied Powers. Although Brüning faced the brunt of this pressure when he became Chancellor a fortnight after the formal acceptance of the Young Plan by the Reichstag on 12 March 1930, Müller's difficulties pointed the way. The more open conflict of class interests (already 2.5 million were unemployed in the winter of 1928–29 and over 3 million the following winter) hardened reactions on all sides and made it increasingly difficult to repair the damage being done to parliamentary institutions [154]. Constant bargaining and nego-tiations accompanied each successive effort to find an agreed legislative basis from which to tackle the economic crisis. Hence the failure of first Rudolf Hilferding, the SPD Minister of Finance, and subsequently Paul Moldenhauer, of the DVP, to frame acceptable proposals. Moldenhauer's suggestions early in 1930 might have temporarily solved the problem by including, among other pro-visions, the raising of the contributions for unemployment insurance from 3.5 to 4 per cent. However, it was precisely over this issue that the DVP and SPD refused to budge from their respective class interests. The former insisted on rigid economies in unemployment relief whilst the latter, notwithstanding Müller's efforts, stubbornly resisted what was felt to be an attack on the very principle of social welfare [26]. Müller eventually admitted defeat when it became quite clear that Hindenburg would not back his government with emergency powers. With the return of the SPD to opposition went the last chance to form a democratic government with a parliamentary majority.

Heinrich Brüning, still only forty-six, a former front-line officer in the First World War, who had risen rapidly in politics to become leader of the Reichstag faction of the Centre Party in 1928, took up the Chancellorship during a period in Germany of profound public disillusionment with the parliamentary system. He headed a minority government containing representatives of the parties of the Great Coalition except for the SPD. Ever since his appointment, Brüning's actions have been the subject of heated debate [19; 26]. Much of the argument has turned on his dissolution of the Reichstag in July 1930, following the repudiation of his government's programme for tackling the economic and financial crisis by 256 to 193 votes. In dissolving parliament, Brüning opened the way for the staggering NSDAP electoral successes in the September elections. Those who have criticised his fateful decision and his subsequent reliance on Article 48 to govern by emergency decrees insist that he threw away other chances to secure a working majority, in particular that of accepting the eventual overtures from the SPD to compromise over details in the legislative programme [3]. It might well be asked, however, how long such a compromise would have lasted. Brüning was certainly constrained by the fact that President Hindenburg was only prepared, in the last resort, to back a rightist government with emergency powers [21]. This reality was barely concealed by terms like 'presidential cabinet' or 'cabinet above the parties'. The bias of the government was all too plain to see from Brüning's protectionist policy towards agriculture, effected with the DNVP Minister for Agriculture, Dr Schiele. His measures kept the price of bread and cereals abnormally high during a period of ruthless economies and cutbacks in public expenditure.

In any event, the class conflict continued to haunt Brüning as it had Müller. Moldenhauer, Brüning's first Minister of Finance, was compelled to resign in the face of the refusal of his own party (DVP) to accept his proposals, in June 1930, for increases in taxation. One of the fundamentals of a relatively stable parliamentary system in the Republic, namely a willingness to compromise between the bourgeois parties and the Social Democrats, had apparently ceased to exist when Brüning took office. Yet a rapid solution to the fiscal crisis was essential, with the budget deficit soaring from 400 million marks in April to 1.1 billion at the end of May [39]. Thus, the dissolution of the Reichstag may well have been the undesirable but probable outcome of Brüning accepting in the first instance the unenviable task of heading a 'presidential government', even though the new Chancellor was personally predisposed towards an authoritarian approach to Germany's problems. This involved securing the support of moderate rightist opinion in Germany and even leaving the way open for an eventual restoration of the monarchy. The strategy also aimed to capitalise on the members of the DNVP who had been driven to leave the party in the face of Hugenberg's extremism and who had formed themselves into the Conservative People's Union under Gottfried Treviranus. Generals Wilhelm Groener and Kurt von Schleicher, as well as President Hindenburg, hoped that the Conservative People's Union might grow into the 'big nationalist, though co-operative party that was their dream' [23 *p. 650*; 188]. Casting his net towards the more moderate right – and this again meant keeping the support of the DVP – also made Brüning reluctant to reinforce his authority by merging the Reich government with that of Prussia, which was still based on the 'Weimar coalition'. A number of historians have argued that Brüning's scepticism about formulating constructive policies with the SPD was not entirely unfounded at that point [112; 120].

Be that as it may, the election results of 14 September 1930 dramatically changed the situation. Brüning's hopes for extending his parliamentary base towards the right were dashed by the fact that the Conservative People's Union returned only four members, by the continued refusal of Hugenberg to co-operate (although his party lost thirty-two seats), and, of course, by the massive surge of support for the NSDAP, which now had 107 seats in the Reichstag. The panic flight to political extremes in reaction to the crisis was confirmed by the gains of the KPD as well as by the losses of the DVP and Democrats, a point which will be further clarified shortly, as will the failure of the government to attract the support of the new voters. In effect, Brüning was now forced to race against time and mounting pressure from the extreme right. His prime aim was not to crush the NSDAP by a frontal assault, which Schleicher would not have permitted [225], nor to involve them in government. Instead, he embarked, with some courage, on his plans for financial and constitutional reform, banking on undermining the appeal of extremists by restoring order and sanity [79]. He was at first reasonably secure in the support of the President and *Reichswehr*, whilst in the Reichstag the SPD's alarm at the Nazi breakthrough led them to adopt the policy of 'toleration' towards Brüning. This was intended to absolve the SPD leaders from any direct responsibility for the harsh policies put forward by the new government, but their toleration, in effect, ensured that the Reichstag would ratify the decrees which Brüning issued with greater frequency [*Doc. 12b*].

Brüning's remedy for tackling the crisis rested on a rigid economic orthodoxy and was bound to be harsh. He sought to offset the effects of falling tax receipts and to cut expenditure, as well as find additional sources of revenue. As a result, some ten new taxes were imposed, and the salaries and pensions of government employees had been drastically reduced, in three stages, by the end of December 1931. General price cuts of 10 per cent were also implemented. Expenditure cuts in social insurance benefits were increased and wages were pegged to the levels of 1927. The attempts to balance the budget had the effect of cutting down production to 60 per cent of what it had been in 1928. That alone helps to explain the catastrophic figure of five million unemployed by early 1931. The one-sided policy of deflation was at least in part due to the restrictions of the Young Plan against devaluing German currency, although financial orthodoxy at the time also favoured the policy [147; 149]. Moreover, there was an insoluble link between Brüning's external and internal policies.

Brüning's deflationary policy was also aimed at highlighting Germany's incapacity to pay reparations and to rid the Republic of a burdensome obligation. Success in this area was seen as vital in making more palatable his government's severe domestic measures, particularly since popular resentment in Germany was being fanned by the 'National Opposition'. Brüning was ultimately dependent in matters concerning reparations on the goodwill of the Allied Powers. These were alarmed, however, by Brüning's demonstrative efforts to appeal to the rising tide of German nationalism, as shown in his espousal of the abortive Austro-German customs union – the forbidden *Anschluss* in poor disguise – and his effort to achieve parity with the Allied Powers for German armaments. It was arguably Utopian to expect to satisfy the National Opposition by concessions to militant revisionism, since for nationalists the continuing attack on Versailles was but part of their vendetta against the government [198]. Yet Brüning himself hardly created this dilemma. Ultimately, he was only able to secure relief over reparations through the Hoover moratorium on inter-governmental debts on 20 June 1931, and this only after the alarming flight of capital from Germany. Some 3.5–4 billion marks worth of gold and foreign currency left the country between September 1930 and July 1931. It was not until after Brüning's fall that reparations were effectively ended, following the Lausanne Conference in July 1932 [136]. In December of that year, Germany's right to equality of armaments was also finally acknowledged [222].

Brüning's tragedy was that, however near to success he came in his own terms, his policies also helped to sustain the conditions in which extremist opposition flourished. This in turn alienated Hindenburg, the *Reichswehr* leaders and the other powerful forces of German conservatism. The significance of this remark can be appreciated by examining these years from the viewpoint of Adolf Hitler and his movement.

More than any other party, the NSDAP depended on the crisis for its successful growth. The official membership statistics for 1935 show an increase from 129,000 to 849,000 between 1930 and the end of January 1933 [5]. During the crisis years the national socialists also recruited a private army for the SA which reached nearly 300,000 men [184]. The election results clearly revealed the rapid growth in the appeal of the NSDAP for a wide variety of groups defecting from the older parties, as well as for the large number of young new voters who went to the polls for the first time in 1930. True, the Catholic vote showed its characteristic resistance to Hitler's charms, and the SPD lost relatively little support. However, defections from the nationalist camp, the DVP and the smaller parties representing interest groups all showed the 'panic of the middle-classes' so often remarked in general studies of Nazism [3 *p. 106*] and long since confirmed by regional voting analyses [179; 186]. Sociological studies of party membership after 1930 confirm the pattern emerging prior to this. No fewer than 43 per cent of new members entering the party between 1930 and 1933 were aged between eighteen and thirty, and 27 per cent between thirty and forty years old. The preponderance of the *petit-bourgeois* social groups was particularly striking. White-collar workers, artisans, merchants, shopkeepers, civil servants and so forth were twice as strongly represented in the NSDAP than in proportion to their position in society as a whole [175; 212]. Although manual workers were markedly under-represented, the party none the less had some success in attracting working-class support. Admittedly, of the 270,000 workers who did join the party before 1933, 120,000 to 150,000 were unemployed [172; 204]. In the universities, too, the national socialists made great gains [213; 215].

The party derived, in particular, enormous benefit from its continued effort to win over the rural population during the crisis. In general, the countryside fell more easily to the Hitler movement than the larger industrial areas and towns, for on the land even the isolated bankrupt had frightening implications for the smaller communities [172]. The success of the NSDAP was striking in Schleswig-Holstein, for example, where between 1928 and 1930 the traditional defender of agrarian interests, the DNVP, fell back from 23 per cent to 6 per cent, whilst the national socialists increased their share of the vote from 4 per cent to 27 per cent. Such figures help to substantiate the assertion that above all 'it was the victims of the crisis, not only the unemployed but the disinherited in general who flocked to the party' [175 *p. 143*; 180; 181]. However, as well as attracting such 'losers', the party enhanced its appeal for the powerful elites in German society. The movement began to attract the attention of the great landowners, for whom Hitler now had a different face and for whom the NSDAP was the lesser evil, as it became clearer that its original programme for land reform would not be implemented. Under the influence of Hitler's skilful words, the great Agrarian League (*Landbund*) proclaimed its intention in January 1931 of henceforth co-operating with the national socialists [26; 31].

If the attitude of the industrialists towards Hitler and his movement was initially more reserved, notwithstanding Hitler's efforts to win their support – for example through his celebrated speech to the *Reichsverband der Deutschen Industrie* (National Federation of German Industry) in January 1932 – and notwithstanding the support of individual influential industrialists like Schacht and Fritz Thyssen, businessmen were increasingly disturbed by first Brüning's and then Schleicher's policies, and this tended to work to Hitler's advantage [218].

The conflicting interests of the varied social groups supporting the NSDAP were hardly to be reconciled after 1933, let alone before. In that sense, the party's reluctance to clarify its multi-purpose programme was well-founded. To vote for Hitler was for many, above all, a rejection of the existing system, and an expression of belief that during a worsening crisis the NSDAP offered the only real hope for the sort of change which specific social groups could fondly hope would be in their own interest. Hence the need for Hitler to focus the party's energy and attention more than ever on the task of becoming a government. At the same time this was also an admission of the difficulty of controlling the internal tensions of the movement as it became a truly mass phenomenon. In Hitler's election speeches and in the party's main paper, the *Völkischer Beobachter,* the propaganda themes of anti-semitism and racism, which continued to be at the very heart of the party's ideas system, were deliberately toned down [195]. They gave way to a massive defamation of the government and a concerted attack on the bankrupt parliamentary system. They emphasised the national humiliation of the German state and promised revision and expansion in foreign affairs, as well as pressing the fanatical anti-communist themes so appealing to the German bourgeoisie and higher social groups [5; 214].

Hitler's role as the all-powerful Führer reached its climax with the massive popular votes devoted to him from 1930 onwards, but, as his efforts to woo the agrarian and industrial establishment indicated, there was a potential danger of his 'legal' tactics being undermined by the continuing revolutionary mood running through important sectors of his movement. The latter were inflamed precisely by the party's dramatic growth. The danger was highlighted for Hitler by his continuing difficulties with the SA, over 60 per cent of whose members were permanently unemployed and whose bloody street battles with the communists [170] graphically reflected their desire for revolutionary frontal attacks on the Republic. In the late summer of 1930 Hitler was compelled, after an SA rebellion in Berlin, to assume himself the position of supreme SA leader and subsequently to reappoint Röhm as Chief of Staff of the SA. The loyal *Schutzstaffeln* (SS), under Heinrich Himmler, became a separate force and helped to keep order among the SA, but this hardly solved the problem, and the longer the crisis lasted the more difficult it was for Hitler to restrain the activists [173; 194].

How important this was becomes clear by emphasising that, as in the early years of the movement in Bavaria, the NSDAP was not in a position to accomplish a revolutionary seizure of power based exclusively on national-socialist forces, and at no time was the movement's share of the vote enough to bring it an absolute parliamentary majority. Under these conditions, it was of the utmost importance to Hitler to collaborate with the DNVP in the 'National Opposition', first against the Young Plan and soon, after further meetings between Hitler and Hugenberg in the summer of 1931, against the Weimar system as a whole. This working alliance with the conservative forces in the National Opposition, formalised as it was in the Harzburg Front from October 1931, brought the national socialists money, the respectability they had certainly not had before, and vastly increased opportunities to penetrate the establishment [198]. Despite this support, and although the NSDAP broke into regional governments before 1933 – Thuringia in January 1930 [*Doc. 17*], Braunschweig in late 1930 and Anhalt, Oldenburg, Mecklenburg in 1932 – Prussia held out as the bastion of democracy under its Weimar coalition until after Brüning's fall [25]. Even after the *Länder* elections of April 1932 had undermined most of the remaining moderate governments, the National Opposition gained a majority only in a few small states. Nor could the working partnership between the Centre Party and SPD in the Reichstag be sprung open. Moreover, between 1930 and 1932 the hardening mood in the SPD masses was reflected in the preparations of the *Reichsbanner* to organise a more efficient fighting force. By the end of 1931 the 'Iron Front' had been set up by the SPD, the free trade unions and the workers' sport organisations to oppose the Harzburg Front [5; 26]. Yet fortunately for Hitler, the protection, or at least the tolerance, of the influential conservative forces, so vital to his success, had a more direct influence on events through the exclusive ring of intimates surrounding the ageing President Hindenburg.

This becomes more than obvious by stressing that for Hitler the protestation of 'legality' was specifically directed, as the crisis developed, at securing for himself the authority which Brüning had virtually institutionalised. Hitler wished to head a government appointed by the President and to be entrusted with extraordinary powers under Article 48. For Brüning, perhaps, there was the justification that he was using emergency powers to preserve the 'state of law', since democracy had clearly failed, whereas Hitler would have no such scruples. The fact remains that between 1930 and 1932 the Reichstag passed twenty-nine relatively minor bills, as opposed to 109 emergency decrees that were ratified by the President. The extensive use of these powers even deprived the Reichstag of the supervisory role to which it was entitled under the same Article 48 by the threat and act of dissolution in the event of parliamentary disapproval. A state of affairs originally envisaged as temporary threatened to become habitual. The public at large was thereby accustomed to think in authoritarian terms of a solution to Germany's problems, whilst more power was transferred to the state bureaucracy, where sympathy for the parliamentary tradition was not strong [42].

Of more direct importance was the increase in the influence of the *Reichswehr*. Schleicher's role in having Brüning appointed underlined this influence [*Doc. 21*], as did the fact that in spite of the Chancellor's financial cuts the *Reichswehr* budget did not suffer unduly. Needless to say, the *Reichswehr* leaders viewed the crisis in terms of what arrangement best suited the interests and future of the army. At first the army leaders were distrustful of the NSDAP and feared its hold over the younger officers in particular. Hitler's attraction for them was made clear at the trial in 1930 of three young national-socialist army officers for treason, because of their assertions that part of the army would not oppose the NSDAP. In spite of this, Hitler's profession, when he spoke at the trial of these officers, of following the legal road, was important in changing army attitudes. So, too, were the early contacts between Schleicher and Röhm in the spring of 1931 and the exchanges between Schleicher and Hitler immediately prior to Brüning's fall [*Doc. 18c*]. There remained, too, the attraction of the SA supplementing the forces of the *Reichswehr* in the event both of a feared, if improbable, Polish attack on Germany's borders and of Germany being allowed greater freedom to rearm. By January 1932 Groener had lifted the existing ban on taking NSDAP members into the *Reichswehr*.

These moves revealed the growing acceptance by the *Reichswehr* leaders of the need to involve the NSDAP ultimately in government. This promised at a stroke to bring to an end emergency rule by extending support on the right, thus capitalising on the all too obvious and growing appeal of the national socialists for many Germans. Hitler's own popularity was graphically confirmed in the elections which took place in March 1932 to determine whether or not Hindenburg should have another term of office. In the first vote in March, Hitler's rival candidacy for Reich President brought him some 30 per cent of the votes polled, and Hindenburg just failed to get an absolute majority. Although Hindenburg's position was secured in the second ballot in early April, the old President had become even more susceptible to intrigues against Brüning. The President's support of Brüning's government, with its intensely unpopular policies, had brought him the bitterness of attacks and vilification from the rightist forces formerly supporting him. In this mood Hindenburg was more readily persuaded to accept Schleicher's view that Brüning – with his reliance on the toleration of the SPD – stood in the way of a government which included the NSDAP. Schleicher also disagreed when Groener banned the SA on 13 April 1932. The decision was in response to demands from Prussia and other states in the interests of keeping public order. None the less, Schleicher was against destroying another bridge to the national socialists, and at the end of May his personal influence made itself felt through the forced resignation of both Brüning and Groener [224; 225].

Whilst there may still be arguments about the significance of Brüning's appointment for the fate of the Republic, many agree that his fall removed the last restraints on the NSDAP, in the sense that his successors were preoccupied to a greater or lesser degree with bringing Hitler to the centre of the stage rather than countering his appeal. The moment seemed auspicious enough for Schleicher's plan for a new leadership. Brüning's successor and Schleicher's candidate, Franz von Papen, headed a cabinet whose reactionary composition gained it the title of the 'Cabinet of Barons' and in which Schleicher himself occupied the Ministry of Defence. Shortly afterwards, a step was at last taken to remove the potential threat from the 'bulwark of the Republic', Prussia. With the Reichstag already dissolved on 4 June 1932 in preparation for new elections, and with the repeal of the ban on the SA and SS, the murderous street fights and disorder occasioned largely by NSDAP and KPD activities offered the pretext to suppress the Prussian government by military action on 20 July 1932. How far the SPD leadership had been progressively weakened by its political tactics and outlook was shown by its failure to mobilise a force to resist. This was of decisive importance in a year when politics and elections were fought largely on the streets. The election of 31 July 1932 again brought staggering successes for the national socialists, who gained over 13.5 million votes and 230 Reichstag seats. Whilst the Centre Party and SPD remained firm in the face of both NSDAP and KPD gains, the bourgeois parties were virtually eliminated as a political force [124) [*Doc. 23*].

It was precisely at this stage that Hitler's gambler's instinct was put to its severest test. The logic of his movement demanded as ever that he control any government of which he was a part. This was not what either Schleicher or von Papen had in mind, and so Hitler remained for the moment outside the charmed circle. Hindenburg, who had allowed Hitler to speak to him on 13 August 1932, was quite against allowing him to head a cabinet with presidential powers. The President was also incensed by Hitler's failure to support von Papen's government [238]. In the event, it was von Papen's own lack of popularity and his inability to control the Reichstag in the face of KPD and NSDAP opposition tactics that worked in Hitler's favour. This was not by any means immediately apparent, for once von Papen was compelled to dissolve the Reichstag disturbing incidents took place in Berlin before voters went to the polls. A strike of Berlin transport workers against the government was supported with violence, not only by the KPD but by the NSDAP, hoping to underline its own opposition to the forces of reaction. The unlikely combination was an indication of the pressure building up in the Hitler movement, but, as a historian of fascism aptly pointed out, Germans had 'voted for Hitler to protect them from Bolshevism, not to bring it closer' [175 *p. 149*]. The November election results at last showed the beginning of a swing away from the NSDAP, whilst middle-class doubts were reflected in the slight recovery of the DNVP and DVP. The KPD increased its votes, but the sudden check to the hitherto continuous growth of the national socialists, and the signs that the economic crisis had passed the worst stages, combined to produce acute depression among the top NSDAP leaders, who were also aware of their party's financial difficulties [5].

In spite of these setbacks, the NSDAP was still the largest party. To govern without the national socialists and its nationalist allies was therefore quite impossible. Hindenburg continued to resist the idea of Hitler heading the government, and the latter remained adamant that he would only join a cabinet as its leader. Von Papen suggested the alternative of dissolving the Reichstag once more and suppressing not only the KPD and NSDAP but other political organisations as a prelude to sweeping constitutional reforms. This was not a practical option, given Schleicher's fear that the army would be damaged by any such venture. The general broke yet another government by convincing Hindenburg of this danger and reluctantly, but logically, himself became Chancellor on 2 December 1932 [224]. The fact remained that Schleicher would be no more successful than von Papen unless he could win over at least a percentage of the NSDAP. Schleicher's failure to achieve this by exploiting the rivalry between Hitler and Gregor Stresser made his position more insecure. Moreover, he had lost goodwill in powerful quarters through his attempt to placate the trade unions by considering employment programmes and repealing von Papen's anti-labour legislation. As a result, leading businessmen and agrarian leaders were more inclined to look favourably on the national socialists. Following Hitler's meeting with the still resentful von Papen at the house of the banker von Schroeder on 4 January 1933, valuable financial contributions were made to the NSDAP by the worried leaders of German industry.

The 'suicidal' readiness of the powerful conservative establishment to hand over key powers to the revolutionary movement led by Hitler was one of the most essential preconditions of his access to supreme power [36; 192]. In some respects it is not really surprising that it should have manifested itself most decisively at the very moment the national socialists were showing signs of decline. These signs may have reinforced the selfish and at best naive hope that, if harnessed to a coalition with other nationalist forces, the NSDAP could be effectively controlled in the interests of social classes whose very survival after the revolution of November 1918 was increasingly felt to be incompatible with the existence of a Republic. In short, the Hitler movement offered the hope of sweeping changes and the eclipse of Bolshevism, whilst permitting the German bourgeoisie at the same time to rest assured that order and property would be preserved – a sort of painless revolution of the right [201].

Who was to prevent this? Hardly the weakened and demoralised forces of the German working classes, nor the army, after Schleicher had been replaced by leaders still more ready to accept Hitler's views. Once the aggrieved von Papen had begun to use the weapons of intrigue against the man who had developed them, Schleicher, it was possible to remove the last remaining obstacle to Hitler's entry into the government, namely Hindenburg's resistance. The President, who was very much in favour of von Papen in any event, was more readily influenced by the accession of his own son, Oscar, to the von Papen camp and grasped at the apparent chance of creating at last a government which would not be isolated from large sectors of German society. Hitler became Chancellor on 30 January 1933, in harness with Hugenberg's nationalists, flanked by von Papen as Vice-Chancellor and apparently comfortably shackled. To subscribe to this astonishing illusion was to overlook what Hitler and his followers had been saying for years, to forget the weakened and divided state of the Reichstag parties, which now had to contend with Hitler's deliberate plans to consolidate his personal position, to dismiss or willingly to ignore the dangers of Article 48 being exploited once Hitler was at the very centre of government, and to underestimate how many Germans were by this time utterly impatient of changing governments and political intrigues. How much this cumulative process owed to the decades before the Republic was even founded can only have been hinted at in this short study, but it is still essential to give weight, not only to the nature of German problems between 1918 and 1929, but to the quite specific series of events between 1929 and 1933 in order to counter the assumption that somehow the Republic was doomed from birth and that Hitler's triumph was predestined. 'The disintegration of the Weimar Republic and the rise of Nazism were two distinct if obviously overlapping historical processes. By 1932, the collapse of Weimar had become inevitable; Hitler's triumph had not' [36 *p. 204*].

PART FOUR: DOCUMENTS

DOCUMENT 1   USPD VIEW OF POLITICAL STRUCTURE

When the Republic was declared the SPD leaders invited the USPD to join an all-socialist government. The reply, printed here, clearly reveals the effort of Haase and his colleagues in the USPD to ensure that genuine changes would take place in the economic, political and social structure of Germany.

To your communication of 9 November 1918 we reply as follows: The USPD is prepared, in order to strengthen the revolutionary socialist gains, to enter the cabinet under the following conditions. The cabinet may only be composed of Social Democrats, who stand together equally empowered as Peoples' Commissars.

This limitation does not apply to the experts; they are merely technical assistants of the executive cabinet. Each of them will have alongside him two members of the Social Democratic parties, one from each party. There will be no condition for delay attached to the entry of the USPD in the cabinet (to which each party sends three members).

Political power lies in the hands of the Workers' and Soldiers' councils, which are to be called together in a plenary Congress from the whole Reich as soon as possible.

The question of the Constituent Assembly will only become actual after the conditions created by the revolution are consolidated and should thus be reserved for later discussions.

In the event of these conditions being accepted, which are dictated from the desire for a united advance of the proletariat, we have delegated to the cabinet our members Haase, Dittmann and Barth.

(Signed HAASE)

From '*Vorwärts*', 11 November 1918, cited in G.A. Ritter and S. Miller, eds, *Die Deutsche Revolution 1918–1919*, Fischer Bücherei, Frankfurt am Main, 1968, p. 83.

DOCUMENT 2   THE PROGRAMME OF THE SPD

The growing rift between the SPD and USPD led to the departure of the latter from government on 29 December 1918. On that same day the following declaration was addressed to the public.

To the German people!
Workers! Soldiers! Citizens! Citizenesses!
The Independents have left the government. The remaining members of the Cabinet vacated their posts so that the Central Council could have a wholly free hand. The latter unanimously re-instated them. The crippling disunity is at an end. The Reich government is reconstructed and united. It professes but one principle: the well being, the survival, the indivisibility of the German Republic above all party interest. On the unanimous recommendation of the Central Council two members of the Social Democratic Party, Noske and Wissell, have replaced the three Independents who resigned. All Cabinet members are equal. Chairmen are Ebert and Scheidemann. And now for our programme. At home:

to prepare for the National Assembly, urgently attend to feeding (the people), initiate socialisation ..., deal severely with war profiteering, create jobs and support the unemployed, improve dependants' relief, to develop the people's army with all means and to disarm unauthorised (personnel). Abroad:

to achieve peace as quickly and as favourably as possible and to re-staff the foreign representations of the German Republic with men imbued with the new spirit. That is the broad outline of our programme prior to the National Assembly.

It will be effected in close contact with the German free states. Its execution will be evident not in words but in deeds. Now we have the opportunity to act! It would be our fault alone if we failed to avail ourselves of it! We must set to! But you must work with us! The new Republic belongs to all of us. Help to secure it! The question raised by the Central Council is also directed at you:

> 'Are you able to defend peace and order against violent attacks and to guarantee the Government's work with all means available against violence, no matter from which side it is perpetrated?'

You must answer this question with a *Yes*! The government has done so without qualification. Without this *Yes*! the programme will remain paper and words! We want to go beyond appeals to *action*! We are getting down to work! We believe in you and in ourselves! *We will win through*!

The government of the Reich: Ebert. Scheidemann. Landsberg. Noske. Wissell.

'*Vorwärts*' No. 358, 30 December 1918. Printed in G.A. Ritter, S. Miller, eds, *Die Deutsche Revolution 1918–1919*, pp. 158–9.

DOCUMENT 3   USPD DEMANDS FOR ACTION

By the time this programme was prepared, the Spartacist 'rising' had been crushed, the elections to the National Assembly had been held and there was no chance of any government implementing the terms proposed in the following extract. Yet it serves as a reminder of the sort of society that might have been created by the revolution.

The immediate demands of the USPD are:

1. Inclusion of the Councils system in the constitutions. Decisive participation of the Councils in legislation, state and municipal government and in industry.

2. Complete dissolution of the old army. Immediate dissolution of the mercenary army made up of volunteer corps (*Freikorps*). Disarming of the bourgeoisie. The setting up of a people's army from the ranks of the class conscious working sector. Self government for the people's army and election of officers by the ranks. The lifting of military jurisdiction.

3. The nationalisation of capitalist undertakings is to begin at once. It is to be executed immediately in the sphere of mining, and of energy production (coal, water-power, electricity), of concentrated iron and steel production as well as of other highly developed industries and of banking and insurance. Landed property and great forests are to be transferred to the community at once. Society has the task of bringing the whole economy to its highest degree of efficiency by making available all technical and economic aids as well as promoting co-operative organisations. In the towns all private property is to pass to the municipality and sufficient dwellings are to be made available by the municipality on its own account.

4. Election of authorities and judges by the people. Immediate setting up of a Supreme Court of Judicature which is to bring to account those responsible for the world war and the prevention of a more timely peace.

5. Any growth of wealth achieved during the war is to be removed by taxation. A portion of all larger fortunes is to be given to the state. In addition public expenditure is to be covered by a sliding scale of income, wealth and inheritance taxes ....

6. Extension of social welfare. Protection for mother and child. War widows, orphans and wounded are to be assured a trouble free existence. Homeless are to be given the use of the spare rooms of owners. Fundamental reorganisation of public health system.

7. Separation of state and church and of church and school. Public, standardised schools with secular character, to be developed according to socialist educational principles. The right of every child to an education corresponding to his ability and availability of the means necessary for this end ....

Extract from the revolutionary programme of the Independent German Social Democratic Party (USPD), 6 March 1919, in J. Hohlfeld, ed.,

Dokumente der deutschen Politik und Geschichte vom 1848 bis zur Gegenwart. Dokumentation-Verlag, Herbert Wendler, Berlin, 1951, vol. 3, pp. 24–5.

DOCUMENT 4   GERMAN DISCUSSION OF PEACE TERMS

After the elections to the National Assembly, a coalition was formed from the SPD, the Democrats and the Centre Party. The new government, headed by the Social Democrat Chancellor, Philipp Scheidemann, had to deal with many complex and urgent problems. This extract is from one of the cabinet meetings which considered the coming terms of peace. The contrast between this reasoned discussion of tactics and the public utterances of the government is marked.

COUNT RANTZAU: Let me make a few preliminary remarks. Our enemies will submit the completed draft (of the peace treaty) with the words 'Take it or leave it'. The draft will diverge widely from Wilson's programme. There are three possibilities: to turn it down; to make a counter proposal; or to examine the draft in detail and make individual counter proposals. The latter is the right approach. Negotiators must be instructed in such a way that they can offer counter proposals. Wilson's programme leaves untouched the question of freedom of the seas as well as the Schleswig question and that of a German-Austrian union. I have divided the material into ten points for the time being: territorial questions; protection of minorities; reparations questions; trade policies; financial questions; general legal questions; German colonies; disarmament; League of Nations; war guilt.

Reparations questions: Rantzau gives further information

ERZBERGER: We must base our arguments on the note of 5 November 1918. After the formal exchange of notes, according to international law, a treaty was concluded. Belgium will have to be completely rebuilt. This does not hold for Northern France. ... The principle for the method of payment must be: small quotas extending over a long period of time. ... There is the possibility that in the long run changes will be made, anyhow. Payment must be in kind, not in money.

DAVID: I agree that we should rest our case on the note of 5 November, but the enemies will have a different interpretation. The note says: 'German attack', not 'German attacks', which means that Germany waged an aggressive war and must make good total damage.

DR BELL: We must take a stand on the guilt question. One might explain that the march through Belgium was motivated by erroneous assumptions. (1) This was an emergency, in which ordinary rules did not apply, and (2) Belgium had a secret agreement with the Entente. We have since realised our mistake. We are, therefore, responsible for repayment of damages.

NOSKE: I still think that in extreme emergencies one fends for oneself as best one can. I cannot even recognise German guilt in Belgium. Nor in U-boat warfare, either – it was a counter measure to starvation blockade. I agree that payments should be spread over a long period.

COUNT RANTZAU: We can justify submarine warfare by the hunger blockade. Other guilt questions will be taken up under point 10.

COUNT BERNSTORFF: The enemies ... will say: 'Besides Wilson's points it must be taken into account that Germany must be punished.' We can reply: '... You only wished to fight to abolish autocracy and militarism and that has been eliminated.' But we won't get anywhere and the big guilt question will still be raised.

GOTHEIN: England and America show understanding for our inability to bear great burdens.

GIESBERTS: We cannot scrape up four billions a year. The standard of living of the German workers and the social welfare measures must be safeguarded. This we must emphasise as a precondition, with reference to the internal political struggle (Bolshevism, etc.).

LANDSBERG: ... The question of guilt and reparations cannot be separated. The march into Belgium resulted from an emergency, but was not self-defence. Emergency conditions do not relieve us from the responsibility for damages, so we should consent to making restitution. The payments should be small.

EBERT: What is the extreme limit of our capacity for reparations payments?

RANTZAU: Does this imply an authorisation to break off negotiations if demands endanger our very existence?

ERZBERGER: Let us maintain, according to the Note of November 5, that reparations be limited to damage in occupied areas. No other demands should be recognized ...

COUNT RANTZAU: I agree. The Reich reparation commission has estimated that on that basis we would have to pay 20 to 25 billions. This takes into account deliveries since the armistice and perhaps colonies given up. This sum is within reason. Payments should be in kind.

SCHIFFER: The principal consideration is what we can pay. Granting that domestic obligations and obligations towards neutrals must be met, hardly any resources are left for payment. ...

BELL: Our negotiators must be clear as to what is the limit of our capacities. ...

COUNT BERNSTORFF: From the legal point of view, we should stick to our interpretation, but we won't be able to put it across, since the English would then not be entitled to reparations, which they keep mentioning in every political statement. ...

EBERT: There is agreement that the note of November 5 in its most favourable interpretation should serve as our starting point.

Extracts from the meeting of the Reich Ministry of 21 March 1919. Reprinted from *Political Institutions of the German Revolution, 1918–1919,*

DOCUMENT 5 A LIBERAL VIEW

When the revolution broke out and the socialists assumed power, the other political parties of the Wilhelmine Empire remained, somewhat stunned, in the background. As it became clearer that the SPD leaders would restore the conditions necessary to hold elections to a National Assembly, the non-socialist parties began to reorganise or to reconstitute themselves to fight those elections. The following extract, written by the editor of the Berliner Tageblatt, *Theodor Wolff, gives some insight into how liberal circles viewed events late in 1918.*

In the afternoon six gentlemen called at my home; three of them I knew and three I had not before met. They were lawyers, industrialists, a professor, and a university lecturer. They wanted me to take the lead in founding a great Democratic middle class party, and expressed the opinion that on account of my attitude during the war I was in the best position to do this. I had no desire to enter into the question whether they were justified in their confidence in me, but already yesterday and today I had been considering the same plan, and since the deputation consisted of people of distinction, and indecision would have been the worst of all things at the moment, I consented. The middle class is frightened and at its wits' end, not knowing what to do or where to turn; most of them are fluttering like birds who have fallen out of the nest and do not know where to go. They must be found another nest, and those who are simply asking all the time 'What is to happen now?' must be given the courage that comes to them only with being in a numerous company and having something to lean on. For a new free state it is possible so far to count on the Social Democracy and the Centre, and that is numerically a great deal, but not enough. The Social Democracy and Catholicism are incontestably two forces of immense importance, and at present the two of the greatest importance. They not only have great hosts at their back but are now the only compact and well knit bodies in the country. But Germany is Germany and anybody with his eyes open and able to look ahead cannot accept these two strong pillars as enough in the long run to give the needed support to a republic – for the Republic has become the only possible thing. Whether it will have a long life in any case is impossible to say as yet, but if at birth it has only a Social Democratic and a Catholic godfather it will be burdened from the outset with a mass of discontent and hostility, and it will be discredited for almost all who might be won over to it from other camps. Thus it is necessary now to organise those strata of the non-Catholic middle class who are all inclined towards democratic ideas, in view of the elections to a National Assembly which it must be hoped will take place – even if it has to be admitted that not everything is good metal that is thus welded together. Naturally large numbers of people will cling to this life-line only in order to escape from the mortal danger that seems to threaten them.

Theodor Wolff, *Through Two Decades*, Heinemann, London, 1936, pp. 138–9.

DOCUMENT 6   **WEIMAR ELECTION RESULTS**

	19 Jan 1919	6 June 1920	4 May 1924	7 Dec 1924	20 May 1928	14 Sep 1930	31 July 1932	6 Nov 1932
Totals on register (in mills)	36.8	35.9	38.4	39.0	41.2	43.0	44.2	44.4
Percentage of voters	82.7	79.1	77.4	78.8	75.6	82.0	84.0	80.6
NSDAP								
Seats	–	–	32	14	12	107	230	196
Per cent	–	–	6.6	3.0	2.6	18.3	37.4	33.1
DNVP								
Seats	44	71	95	103	73	41	37	52
Per cent	10.3	15.1	19.5	20.5	14.2	7.0	5.9	8.8
DVP								
Seats	19	65	45	51	45	30	7	11
Per cent	4.4	14.0	9.2	10.1	8.7	4.5	1.2	1.9
Centre & BVP								
Seats	91	85	81	88	78	87	98	90
Per cent	19.7	17.9	15.6	17.3	15.1	14.8	15.9	15.0
DDP								
Seats	75	39	28	32	25	20	4	2
Per cent	18.6	8.3	5.7	6.3	3.8	3.6	1.0	1.0
SPD								
Seats	165	102	100	131	153	143	133	121
Per cent	37.9	21.6	20.5	26.0	29.8	24.5	21.6	20.4
USPD								
Seats	22	84						
Per cent	7.8	17.9	0.8					
KPD								
Seats	–	4	62	45	54	77	89	100
Per Cent	–	2.1	12.6	9.0	10.6	14.3	14.6	16.9
Number of deputies in the Reichstag	421	459	472	493	491	577	608	584
Votes cast in millions	30.4	28.2	29.3	30.3	30.8	35.0	36.9	35.5

The figures given for the NSDAP in 1924 are those of the racialists. G. Castellan [8], p. 117.

DOCUMENTS 7a, b, c   OSTPOLITIK

According to the Treaty of Versailles, Germany was compelled to recognise future, as yet unspecified, Allied arrangements for Russia. However, the following document indicates the possibility of Germany exploiting the ambiguity of some of the Versailles clauses. The memorandum was composed during the course of the Soviet-Polish war, towards which Germany's official policy was one of neutrality. This policy, in effect, benefited Russia rather than the Poles.

[a]

Germany is so far limited in the independence of its Eastern policy by the Treaty of Versailles that it must recognize in advance the settlement of Eastern questions intended by the Entente. So far, in theory, it can conclude with Russia, as with Latvia, only a 'provisional' agreement; also it cannot undertake any alteration of the terms of the Treaty of Versailles, in agreement with Russia, which (country) in this respect is quite unhindered. ... It is up to Russia to make any provisional treaty which is concluded durable, by allowing ... the Entente no decisions which oppose the agreement concluded or to be concluded with Germany, which the growing position of power of Russia *vis-à-vis* the Entente makes possible. For this reason the priority of the German-Russian negotiations is of significance and suspicions which could arise against these (negotiations) beginning in view of German neutrality must be rejected. Economic negotiations are not a breach of neutrality.

Auswärtiges Amt. Files, Akten betreffend Verhandlungen mit Sowjet Russland (Graf Mirbach, Ostschutz) Politik 2 Russland, Bd 1, Foreign Office Microfilm, K281/K095960–K095962, London.

Memorandum of the Russian Section of the German Foreign Office dated 13 August 1920.

Many influential Germans and government officials in the Weimar Republic were enthusiastic about Germany making a full recovery through the help of Russia. Even the Chief of the Reichswehr, Hans von Seeckt, insisted on the primacy of German-Russian relations, as this extract indicates.

[b]

Poland's existence is intolerable, incompatible with the survival of Germany. It must disappear, and it will disappear through its own internal weakness and through Russia – with our assistance. For Russia Poland is even more intolerable than for us; no Russian can allow Poland to exist. With Poland falls one of the strongest pillars of the Treaty of Versailles, the preponderance of France. ... Poland can never offer any advantage to Germany, either economically, because it is incapable of any development, or politically, because it is France's vassal. The re-establishment of the broad common frontier between Russia and Germany is the precondition for the regaining of strength of both countries. 'Russia and Germany within the frontiers of 1914!' should be the basis of reaching an understanding between the two. ...

We aim at two things: first, a strengthening of Russia in the economic and political, thus also in the military field, and so indirectly a strengthening of ourselves, by strengthening a possible ally of the future; we further desire, at first cautiously and experimentally, a direct strengthening of ourselves, by helping to create in Russia an armaments industry which in case of need will serve us. ...

In all these enterprises, which to a large extent are only beginning, the participation and even the official knowledge of the German government must be entirely excluded. The details of the negotiations must remain in the hands of the military authorities. ...

Memorandum by Seeckt, 11 September 1922, in Carsten [225], pp. 140–1.

The recollections of the German Chancellor whose government negotiated the Rapallo agreement remind us that there was also opposition to it.

[c]
Unfortunately, Ebert broke with Rathenau as early as Spring 1922. He remarked to me prior to Rapallo: 'I am fed up with Rathenau and his clique!' Matters were bad after Rapallo. Already in April 1922 Ebert said to me on the subject of the link with Russia: 'How can you associate with these scoundrels ...?' By May 1922 the downfall of the government I led was a forgone conclusion. Quite soon after the death of Rathenau I offered my resignation to Ebert. 'Try on another occasion!' was the response of the now very mistrustful Ebert.

Letter from Wirth to Dr Otto Braun, 22 July 1941, printed in H. Schulze, 'Rückblick auf Weimar. Ein Briefwechsel zwischen Otto Braun and Josph Wirth im Exil', *Vierteljahrshefte für Zeitgeschichte*, 1978, p. 168.

DOCUMENT 8   **STRESEMANN AND *WESTPOLITIK***

In practice, German governments followed a cautious line in relations with Soviet Russia, particularly once Stresemann had taken over the conduct of foreign policy from 1923. He was anxious to maintain good working relations with a Russia he personally did not greatly like, but his major effort was directed at achieving an understanding with the western powers. A major step in this direction was Germany's entry to the League of Nations following the Locarno treaties of 1925.

My father left Berlin on the evening of 8 September (1926) at the head of a delegation comprising members of parliament, representatives of the Reich Chancellor and the Prussian Minister President as well as officials from the *Auswärtiges Amt.* Chancellor Marx himself remained in Berlin, since the other great powers were also represented only by their foreign ministers. Finally the treaty of Locarno was in force, after a period of grumbling and arguments on both sides, once because of Allied complaints about incidents in the occupied territories and also on account of the scale of the reduction of the occupying forces. The mood in which my father found himself then and indeed later is perhaps best revealed from an address he made before the foreign press at the end of June and where among other things he said: '... I am convinced that we are by no means finished with the clash of opinions and that generally there can be no advance without setbacks ... It is also true of Locarno that the sunshine in this delightfully beautiful corner of the world will be followed by gloomy days in all countries. It has become apparent everywhere that the bold initiatives and the co-operation of leaders meet considerable scepticism and doubt from the peoples and their representatives. ... The struggle in my own country is God knows hard, but I am convinced of one thing – and that entitles me to feel confident – that human progress can only be founded on the idea of peace, that this alone can conquer the hearts of mankind, and this conviction comes from my personal acquaintance with and my knowledge of European politics. ... I am also convinced that the achievement of Locarno must be the foundation of foreign policy in future ... (there are) routes which we embarked on in the belief that the earth on which we dwell is condemned to sterility if it does not find the path towards the policy of peace, towards the idea of friendship which acknowledges that the fate of humankind does not end at the borders of the different countries and nations. ... It is less a matter of clauses, than of the general spirit of the treaties. ... If the ideas win through, the clauses will no longer divide nations. Therefore nothing is more mistaken than to assume that the spirit of Locarno depends solely on fulfilling certain stipulations. ...'

W. Stresemann, *Mein Vater Gustav Stresemann,* 2nd enlarged edition, Frankfurt, Ullstein, 1985, pp. 423–4.

DOCUMENT 9   CHANCELLOR MARX ON FOREIGN POLICY

When Marx formed his fourth cabinet early in January 1927, he brought in the Nationalists on the condition that they accepted Stresemann's continuation in office as Foreign Minister. This hardly led the DNVP to abandon its hostility towards Versailles or towards the principle of co-operating with the Allied Powers, but it enabled Marx to offer the following announcement to the Reichstag.

In no other sphere is the continuity of governmental aims to a greater degree the prerequisite of fruitful work than in the sphere of foreign policy. This continuity is the basis of international confidence. Germany would immeasurably increase the difficulties of its position if the organic development of its policy towards the other countries were damaged by changes in internal politics. So it is self-evident that the government will further develop the existing foreign policy in the sense of mutual understanding. This line is clearly and unequivocally identifiable from the decisions taken with the consent of the constitutional authorities in recent years. The foreign policy which the Reich government has pursued unceasingly and unflinchingly since the end of the war and which ultimately led to the London Dawes Agreement, to the treaties of Locarno and to entry into the League of Nations, is characterised by a rejection of the notion of revenge. Its purpose is rather the achievement of a mutual understanding. Whatever may have been the standpoint of individual parties in the past, for the future the only appropriate development can be that indicated, on the foundations this achieved. ...

Extract from the government declaration of Chancellor Marx before the Reichstag on 2 February 1927. J. Hohlfeld, ed., *Dokumente der deutschen Politik und Geschichte vom 1848 bis zur Gegenwart*, Dokumentation-Verlag, Herbert Wendler, Berlin, 1951, vol. 3, p. 171.

DOCUMENT 10   DOMESTIC IMPACT OF INFLATION

When the French occupied the Ruhr in January 1923, to force Germany to meet her reparations payments, the ensuing economic and monetary crisis produced shocking and lasting effects on large sectors of German society, as the following two documents 10 and 11 demonstrate.

May I give you some recollections of my own situation at that time? As soon as I received my salary I rushed out to buy the daily necessities. My daily salary, as editor of the periodical *Soziale Praxis*, was just enough to buy one loaf of bread and a small piece of cheese or some oatmeal. On one occasion I had to refuse to give a lecture at a Berlin City college because I could not be assured that my fee would cover the subway fare to the classroom, and it was too far to walk. On another occasion, a private lesson I gave to the wife of a farmer was paid somewhat better – by one loaf of bread for the hour.

An acquaintance of mine, a clergyman, came to Berlin from a suburb with his monthly salary to buy a pair of shoes for his baby; he could buy only a cup of coffee. The Zeiss works in Jena, a nonprofit enterprise, calculated the gold mark equivalent of its average wage paid during a week in November 1923 and found weekly earnings to be worth four gold marks, less than a sixth of prewar levels.

Personal memoir of Dr Frieda Wunderlich, cited in Bry [139], p. 55.

DOCUMENT 11   HEALTH AND THE COST OF LIVING

In the session of the Prussian legislature for January 23, the Prussian Minister of Welfare, drawing upon the report submitted for Prussia, has already given us a picture of the most grievous want and deep misery in matters of health in that state.

Unfortunately, this picture of accelerating and shocking decline in health conditions applies to the whole Reich. In the rural areas where many self-sufficient farmers are able to feed themselves and the difficulties resulting from a great density of population do not exist, conditions seem to be better. But in the towns and in the districts with an industrial mass population, there has been a decided deterioration. Especially hard-hit are the middle class, those living on small annuities, the widows and the pensioners, who with their modest incomes can no longer afford the most basic necessities at present day prices. It is going just as badly for those who cannot yet earn. I mention students only as an example. The expense of even the most essential foodstuffs – I need only indicate fats, meat and bread – and the want of coal, linen, clothing and soap, prevent any improvement in living conditions. The height to which prices have climbed may be shown by the fact that as of February 15, wholesale prices have risen on the average to 5967 times the peacetime level, those of foodstuffs to 4902 times, and those for industrial products to 7958 times. Meat consumption has fallen from 52 kilograms per person in 1912 to 26 kilograms per person in 1922. In the occupied zone, moreover, this small amount has presumably to be shared with many foreign mouths as well. For many people, meat has become altogether a rarity. A million and a half German families are inadequately provided with fuel. Thousands upon thousands of people spend their lives jammed together in the most primitive dwellings and must wait for years before they can be assigned quarters which satisfy even the most elementary hygienic requirements. ...

It is understandable that under such unhygienic circumstances, health levels are deteriorating ever more seriously. While the figures for the Reich as a whole are not yet available, we do have a preliminary mortality rate for towns with 100,000 or more inhabitants. After having fallen in 1920–21, it has climbed again for the year 1921–22, rising from 12.6 to 13.4 per thousand inhabitants. In 1922, those familiar diseases appeared again in increasing numbers which attack a people when it is suffering from insufficient nutrition, when it also can no longer obtain the other necessities of life. Thus edema is reappearing, the so-called war dropsy, which is a consequence of a bad and overly watery diet. There are increases in stomach disorders and food poisoning, which are the result of eating spoiled foods. There are complaints of the appearance of scurvy, which is a consequence of an unbalanced and improper diet. From various parts of the Reich, reports are coming in about an increase in suicides. ... More and more often one finds 'old age' and 'weakness' listed in the official records on the causes of death; these are equivalent to death through hunger. Just recently the painful news appeared in the daily press that a well-known German scholar, Professor Hayn of Dresden, has died of hunger.

Extract from a speech by Franz Bumm, President of the Reich Department of Health, before the Reichstag on 20 February 1923, in Ringer [150], pp. 112–13.

DOCUMENTS 12a AND b   **DIVISIONS BETWEEN SOCIALISTS AND COMMUNISTS**

The VI World Congress of Comintern's depiction of Social Democrats as a branch of fascism (Social Fascists) in 1928 damaged prospects for a KPD and SPD 'united front' to counter the growing menace of national socialism, following its spectacular electoral success in September 1930. Divisions were highlighted at mass meetings organised by the KPD and SPD in Berlin, respectively for 8 September and 14 September 1931. KPD spokesman, Heinz Neumann, addressed the latter meeting, as did the SPD's Berlin District Leader, Franz Künstler, His response was coloured by the KPD's participation with the NSDAP in a referendum on 9 August 1931, aimed, unsuccessfully, at bringing down the SPD-led government in Prussia under Otto Braun.

[a]
Franz Künstler: The KPD, which on 9 August made common cause with the German counter-revolution, is not suited to lead the German workers, has no right to criticise Social Democracy. The clamour for a united front is every bit as discreditable as the rest of the KPD's policy. Is this the united front, when the KPD so inflames its followers that the attacks on socialist democrat workers and functionaries mount daily? In the final week alone

before the referendum nine social democratic officers were attacked by communists.

What can Heinz Neumann tell us about the murder of 21-year-old comrade Max Warkus in Leipzig? We don't expect an answer to this question today! Does the KPD approve of the murder of brothers and workers? In the *Neue Welt* Neumann wrote: 'We are prepared to fight with any honest *Reichsbanner* member against the Nazi terror.' But the truth is that communists and Nazis rival one another in organising underhand assaults on *Reichsbanner* workers.

Communist calls for a united front will not distract workers from the fact that on 9 August *Stahlhelm*, Swastika and Red Star joined forces against the Republic and the working classes. This three-way partnership opened the workers' eyes. The referendum initiated by the *Stahlhelm* in conjunction with Hitler and Hugenberg was dubbed a 'red referendum' by the KPD. Only people for whom the penny hasn't dropped could do this. We have a second question for Neumann: When did the KPD ever propose a popular vote or plebiscite? In the *Landtag* on 16 October 1930 communist member Schwenk described a people's referendum as the people's greatest deception. The KPD's attitude is clear from its action and no smearing of social democracy can alter the fact that the German section of the 3rd International participated in an action of the German counter-revolution. (Lively applause)

Künstler then described at length the voting results in the communist strongholds (in Berlin), Wedding, Neuköln and Friedrichshain. A comparison with the outcome of the last Reichstag elections shows that on 9 August the communists had failed to mobilise even half of their supporters for the plebiscite. (Very true!) By contrast and in spite of economic crisis and unemployment suffering, social democracy in Berlin could point to a constant rise in membership. ... The communist camp should not resort to lying from envy, although one can understand their anguish, that the number of Berlin social democrat members alone equals two-thirds of the KPD's total membership in Germany. (Bravo!) ...

It is the tragedy of the German working classes, that they are unable to unite decisively in the most difficult hour ... A year has passed today since the 14 September [1930 elections]. It is the unique achievement of social democracy alone that fascism has not come to power. And you, Herr Neumann, and your Communist Party, are the beneficiaries of German social democracy.

Vorwärts. Berliner Volksblatt, Zentralorgan der Sozialdemokratischen Partei Deutschlands, Vol. 48, 1931, No. 431, 15 September 1931, 1–2. Reprinted in W. Luthardt, ed., *Sozialdemokratische Arbeiterbewegung und Weimarer Republik. Materialen zur gesellschaftlichen Entwicklung 1927–1933*, vol. 2, Suhrkamp, Frankfurt, 1978, pp. 219–21.

[b]

Heinz Neumann: I believe it would have been better, in the interests of social democratic workers, if the SPD's spokesman had addressed the issue of the policy of the Brüning government. Everyone of us here – whether communist or *Reichsbanner* member or social democrat – feels in their own person the impact of this monstrous crisis situation. This gathering is concerned with the method and goal of the proletarian class struggle. (Continuous calls: referendum!) I will talk about the referendum, I shall not duck any question.

But I must affirm: a day before the Prussian government publishes its new emergency decree, a decree bringing burdens totalling another 250 million marks for the working population, on this day, it would have been appropriate for the Social Democratic Party to have made clear through its nominated ward spokesman, what its response is to the emergency decree of the Prussian government.

As to the referendum: we communists regard the Braun–Severing government in Prussia as an executive organ of Brüning's policy.

The Braun–Severing policy is for better or for worse tied with the policy of the Brüning administration. Social democratic ministers have participated in preparing the new emergency measures. And if the Social Democratic Party entered the electoral battle one year ago today with the slogan 'Against Brüning, against the government of Article 48', then I ask you, why is it now in favour of Brüning and for burdening the masses? The Severing–Braun government in Prussia is in our view not one which represents the interests of the worker. The referendum was directed against the Prussian government. You are of the opinion that the Braun–Severing administration in Prussia is a bulwark against fascism. ...

We communists are also republicans (uproar). But the republic we desire is not the republic at whose head stand Brüning and Hindenburg, not the republic whose police chase the unemployed from the streets with rubber truncheons, not the republic of emergency decrees, not the republic where fascist assassins run freely ...

You say: if the Severing government falls, if the Brüning regime collapses, then Hitler will take its place. We say, if that happens then neither Hitler nor Hugenberg but the working class will replace it. (Prolonged applause)

Rote Fahne, vol. 14, 1931, No. 178, 15 September 1931, Appendix 1. Reprinted in W. Luthardt, ed., *Sozialdemokratische Arbeiterbewegung*, pp. 221–5.

DOCUMENT 13   FALSE LEGENDS

*An eminent German historian recalls his own experience of the early
Weimar Republic and gives some idea of how pervasive were the rightist
legends of early post-war Germany.*

I myself am, perhaps, not the worst witness in this matter since I grew up in
the midst of this atmosphere. In our high school in Stuttgart, as indeed, in
most of the secondary schools in Germany after 1918, a noticeable rightist
trend prevailed, which most of the teachers followed, at least those who
spoke to us about politics. We believed that it was the stab in the back
alone that had prevented a German victory; we had one Pan-German
history teacher who defended this worst form of the legend. We were
convinced that one could be patriotic only on the rightist side. We repeated
the stupid jokes, which were then circulating among the middle class, about
President Ebert and his wife, and which were supposed to prove their
unworthiness. In fact, the Eberts succeeded, with quiet dignity, in regaining
a sympathy for Germany under the most trying conditions – in a world in
which public opinion was dominated by Germany's wartime enemies. About
this, however, we heard nothing, and we read nothing about it in our
rightist middle class press. We did not know what the actual situation of the
war had been in 1918; we were taught to hate the French and the British
and to despise the Americans. We were pressed into a form that had
become empty. We did not see that the socialist workers had also sacrificed
their blood for Germany – for a country that had never really given them a
chance. We were not meant to suspect that the leading classes of Imperial
Germany had made serious mistakes, and that these had jeopardised the
victory (if victory had ever been a possibility) as much as the trend on the
left had. We were brought up for a world that no longer existed, and we
took up nationalistic slogans, while the Republic of which we were trying to
make fun was trying to pull the waggon out of the mud.

After graduation, many of our class joined the 'black army'. It was at this
point that I, a student and a student apprentice in Stuttgart, broke through
this form and saw how wrong we were. Thus, at eighteen, I became
immune to the allurements of Hitlerism and could observe the rise of the
Weimar Republic with keen interest.

Fritz Ernst, *The Germans and Their Modern History*, Columbia University
Press, New York, 1966, pp. 47–8.

DOCUMENT 14   THE MURDER OF WALTHER RATHENAU

Although the Freikorps *formations set up in Germany in the immediate post-war years were soon officially dissolved, many of them continued to lead a semi-legal existence. In the following extract, the celebrated German author, Ernst von Salomon, who was a* Freikorps *member, recalls his part in the preliminaries to the murder of the German Foreign Minister, Walther Rathenau.*

I think there are two things which it's important not to confuse. First of all there was the plan, the concept that inspired the deed – and then there were the personal motives that induced the individuals to take part in it. The plan itself, how did that arise? Actually there was only one political common denominator that held the whole 'national movement' together at that time, and it was a negative one: it amounted to this: 'We must make an end to *Erfüllungspolitik*, to the policy of accepting the Versailles Treaty and co-operating with the West.' That was the one point on which all the groups and sub-groups were agreed, though they might and did argue about everything else. We had no wish to become a political party with mass support and all that that implies. We did not wish to use the devil to drive out Beelzebub. But we did, from the very beginning, desire basic change, a 'national revolution' that would free us from the material and ideological supremacy of the West as the French revolution had freed France from its monarchy. So our means had to be different from those of the political parties. I think it was Kern himself – it agreed with his logical temperament – who finally said, during a heated argument, that in that case the only course open was to 'eliminate' every *Erfüllungs* politician. To eliminate in that context is, of course, to kill. What other means were there at our disposal? None of those who were repelled by Kern's conclusions could think of any. And once a group was in existence, a very small group, which was so far in agreement, the rest followed more or less automatically, as it were. The atmosphere in which we proposed to carry out a series of assassinations was not unlike that in which the Russian revolutionary Socialists planned theirs – except for the great difference that their deeds were based on belief in a well thought out political and economic doctrine whereas ours were the product of an emotion. Well, the theories of the Revolutionary Socialists have been only very partially fulfilled. There, as here, subsequent developments were almost automatic. There, as here, 'lists' were drawn up. And on one of our lists, among many others, was Rathenau's name.

'That list!' I said. It was, in fact, a single dirty sheet of paper with names scribbled all over it in pencil, some crossed out, some written in again. Many of the names meant absolutely nothing to me, and I had to take quite a lot of trouble to find out who the people were. Incidentally, Theodor Wolff was on the list. I remember thinking that there were a lot of Jewish names. One name, Wassermann, I crossed out myself because I thought it meant Jacob Wassermann, the writer: in fact it was Oskar Wassermann, the banker, a man of whom I knew nothing. The whole thing was drawn up in a fantastically casual way. I didn't set eyes on it until very much later on, in Berlin, when we were in the midst of our preparations for assassinating Rathenau. Kern had left it lying on a table in the boarding house on the Schiffbauerdamm, which was where we were staying at the time. It was pure chance that I took part in the murder of Rathenau; it happened quite 'automatically', because I had become so attached to Kern.

From *The answers of Ernst von Salomon to the 131 questions in the Allied military government 'Fragebogen'*, Putnam, London, 1954, pp. 55–6.

DOCUMENT 15   THE CHARACTER OF THE NSDAP

Whilst attempting to become a mass movement, the NSDAP remained essentially a conspiratorial group, as is revealed by the sharp distinction made in the following extract between mere supporters and active members of the party organisation.

When a movement harbours the purpose of tearing down a world and building another in its place, complete clarity must reign in the ranks of its own leadership with regard to the following principles.

Every movement will first have to sift the human material it wins into two large groups: supporters and members.

The function of propaganda is to attract supporters, the function of organisation to win members.

A supporter of a movement is one who declares himself to be in agreement with its aims, a member is one who fights for them.

The supporter is made amenable to the movement by propaganda. The member is induced by the organisation to participate personally in the recruiting of new supporters, from whom in turn members can be developed.

Since being a supporter requires only a passive recognition of an idea, while membership demands active advocacy and defence, to ten supporters there will at most be one or two members.

Being a supporter is rooted only in understanding, membership in the courage personally to advocate and disseminate what has been understood.

Understanding in its passive form corresponds to the majority of mankind which is lazy and cowardly. Membership requires an activistic frame of mind and thus corresponds only to the minority of men.

Propaganda will consequently have to see that an idea wins supporters, while the organisation must take the greatest care only to make the most valuable elements among the supporters into members. Propaganda does not, therefore, need to rack its brains with regard to the importance of every individual instructed by it, with regard to his ability, capacity and understanding, or character, while the organisation must carefully gather from the mass of these elements those which really make possible the victory of the moment.

Adolf Hitler, *Mein Kampf* [189], pp. 520–30.

DOCUMENT 16   HITLER'S APPEAL

In his speeches Hitler came back repeatedly to key themes, finding convenient scapegoats on which to focus public resentment in the distress of post-war Germany. More often than not it was the 'Jew' or 'Bolshevik' who was, according to Hitler, the root of Germany's problems. By contrast, the Hitler movement was portrayed as struggling ceaselessly to cut through the jungle of pernicious influences in order to reconstruct a new Germany.

Certainly a government needs power, it needs strength. It must, I might almost say, with brutal ruthlessness press through the ideas which it has recognised to be right, trusting to the actual authority of its strength in the State. But even with the most ruthless brutality it can ultimately prevail only if what it seeks to restore does truly correspond to the welfare of the whole people.

That the so-called enlightened absolutism of a Frederick the Great was possible depended solely on the fact that, though this man could undoubtedly have decided 'arbitrarily' the destiny – for good or ill – of his so-called 'subjects', he did not do so, but made his decisions influenced and supported by one thought alone, the welfare of his Prussian people. It was this fact only that led the people to tolerate willingly, nay joyfully, the dictatorship of the great king.

And the Right has further completely forgotten that democracy is fundamentally not German: it is Jewish. It has completely forgotten that this Jewish democracy with its majority decisions has always been without exception only a means towards the destruction of any existing Aryan leadership. The Right does not understand that directly every small question of profit or loss is regularly put before so-called 'public opinion' he who knows how most skilfully to make this 'public opinion' serve his own interests becomes forthwith master in the State. And that can be achieved by the man who can lie most artfully, most infamously: and in the last resort he is not the German, he is, in Schopenhauer's words, 'the great master in the art of lying' – the Jew.

And finally it has been forgotten that the condition which must precede every act is the will and the courage to speak the truth – and that we do not see today – either in the Right or in the Left.

There are only two possibilities in Germany: do not imagine that the people will for ever go with the middle party, the party of compromises:

one day it will turn to those who have most consistently foretold the coming ruin and have sought to dissociate themselves from it. And that party is either the Left: and then God help us! for it will lead us to complete destruction – to Bolshevism, or else it is a party of the Right which at the last, when the people are in utter despair, when it has lost all its spirit and has no longer any faith in anything, is determined for its part ruthlessly to seize the reins of power – that is the beginning of resistance of which I spoke a few minutes ago. Here, too, there can be no compromise ... and there are only two possibilities: either victory of the Aryan or annihilation of the Aryan and the victory of the Jew.

It is from the recognition of this fact, from recognising it, I would say, in utter, dead earnestness, that there resulted the formation of our Movement.

Speech of 12 April 1922, in *Hitler's Speeches* [190], vol. I, pp. 13–14.

DOCUMENT 17   A NATIONAL SOCIALIST MINISTER IN THE GOVERNMENT OF THURINGIA

Although the NSDAP had to work within the parliamentary framework to win support after 1923, the following extract from one of Hitler's letters is revealing. The remarks refer to the election of Wilhelm Frick as Interior and Education Minister in Thuringia in 1929. His was the first appointment of a national socialist as a minister in one of the German Lands. The extract also shows the continuous effort expended by the party in its so-called lean years.

The parties in Thuringia who had comprised the government hitherto were unable to put a majority together without our co-operation. We could have had a decisive influence earlier – before [Artur] Dinters' [Gauleiter of Thuringia until 1928] departure. However, only the new election gave us the numerical strength to frustrate the formation of an administration without our participation. Moreover, in the meantime there had been a very considerable swing in public opinion. It is astonishing how the usual arrogant, snobbish or idiotic dismissal of the party of a few years ago has changed to an attitude of hopeful expectancy. It was consistent with this transformation therefore that the former ruling parties in Thuringia asked us for the first time to play an active role in the government. I believe it was expected of me (particularly by the German People's Party) that I would make some nationalist-type official available, who could soon be fixed. Therefore on this occasion it was essential to show the Herr Party Politicians from the outset that any attempt at duping the national socialist movement is laughable. Thus I declared my willingness in principle to play an active part in forming the government in Thuringia. Had I said 'no' and had there as a result been another dissolution of the *Landtag*, many voters might have regretted their decision to give us their trust. From the moment I expressed our agreement in principle any new election would have disadvantaged the other parties. After our readiness in principle to participate in the government had been given in this way and accepted, I put two demands: Interior Ministry and Education Ministry. In my view these are the two most important offices for us in the *Lands*. Subordinated to the Interior Ministry is the whole administrative apparatus, the personnel office, and therefore the appointment and dismissal of all officials, as well as the police. Answerable to the Education Ministry is all schooling, from elementary school to the University in Jena, as well as the theatre. Whoever controls these two ministries and ruthlessly and unwaveringly exploits their power can have an exceptional impact. Naturally a precondition of this is a suitable personality. I was certain that no petty parliamentarian or obedient government official could be considered for this position, but only a dyed in the wool national socialist, with an expertise matching his dedication to national socialism. I am fortunate in having such a man in comrade Dr. Frick. ... An energetic and bold officer, ready to assume responsibility, of exceptional ability and a fanatical national socialist! When I informed the representatives of the other government parties of my candidate, there was deep upset to begin with.

Private letter from Hitler, 2 December 1929. Printed in E. Deuerlein, ed., *Der Aufstieg der NSDAP in Augenzeugenberichten*, 3rd edition, Deutscher Taschenbuch Verlag, Munich, 1978, pp. 306–7.

DOCUMENTS 18a, b, c   **THE ARMY IN POLITICS**

The decision of the German military leaders to put themselves at Ebert's disposal to crush Bolshevism saved their own skins and enabled them to carry over into the new Republic much of the spirit and structure of the old German army. This step did not mean that the new army, the Reichswehr, *was any the less opposed to the Republic, but what mattered was to build up a united, disciplined force and to eliminate outside influences as far as possible. The abortive attempt to seize power, made by Wolfgang Kapp in 1920, provided Seeckt, the new head of the* Reichswehr, *with an opportunity to underline the inherent dangers to the* Reichswehr's *position if it became involved in fratricidal conflicts.*

[a]
The Field Marshal and I intend to support Ebert, whom I estimate as a straightforward, honest and decent character, as long as possible so that the cart does not slide further to the left. But where is the courage of the middle class? That a tiny minority could simply overthrow the whole German Empire together with its member states, is one of the saddest events of the

whole history of the German nation. During four years the German people stood unbroken against a world of enemies – now it permits a handful of sailors to knock it down as if it were a dummy ...

Groener's letter to his wife on 17 November 1918, cited in Carsten [225], p. 20.

[b]
There are numerous indications that many members of the Reichswehr do not see clearly into what a situation we have got through the events of March (Kapp Putsch), and that we must take the consequences for the results of our political short-sightedness. ... Although it cannot be denied that the majority of misdemeanours can to some extent be excused on grounds of military obedience, we must nevertheless realise and acknowledge that offences have been committed in our ranks which call for punishment. If we do not admit this ourselves and do not set out on the path of reformation, we must not complain if attempts are made from outside to effect changes. By such offences I not only understand those connected with the political events of the past weeks, but above all the cases of gross indiscipline and brutal behaviour which have occurred in certain units. I do not intend to tolerate or to forget such occurrences. For troops that have tarnished the honour of the soldier there is no room in the Reichswehr. ... We must use all our efforts to eliminate political activity of any kind from the army. ... We do not ask what political opinion the individual has; but I must expect from everybody who continues to serve in the Reichswehr that he takes his oath seriously and has, voluntarily and as an honest soldier, taken his stand on the basis of the constitution ...

Decree of Seeckt of 18 April 1920, in Carsten [225], pp. 105–106.

Behind the following advice given by General von Schleicher to Reich Minister of the Interior, General Groener, lay the former's determination to forge good relations with the SA and the NSDAP, thus preparing the way for a more right-wing government. At the time of writing this letter, in March 1932, Schleicher was trying to persuade Groener not to ban the SA in Prussia, following the raid by the Social Democrat Minister of the Interior, Severing, on Nazi headquarters in Prussia and the evidence he found about the SA's plans for a coup in the event of Hitler winning a majority in the presidential elections, the second ballot of which was scheduled for 10 April.

[c]
Your Excellency
First, [I wish you] many nice Easter eggs, but not the sort of cuckoo eggs which Severing-Badt & Co. have hatched out. ... I am only afraid that my

particular friends in the Reich Ministry of the Interior are themselves not entirely innocent. Basically their aim is to win Your Excellency for the struggle against the Right in the Prussian elections so that you will be branded as a faithfull ally of the Socialists. To achieve this end they regard any means as permissible, such as mysterious hints about the Border Guards to French correspondents [that is, that Germany was evading the Versailles restrictions] and naked threats by the SPD party headquarters and by the Prussian Ministry of the Interior that they will not vote for Hindenburg on 10 April if your Excellency does not take up the struggle against the SA. Naturally, attempts have not been lacking to portray the basically amiable Groener as a victim of the devilish Schleicher. But in the long run that no longer has any effect; the lie is too brazen. I am really looking forward to 11 April – then we will really be able to deal with this pack of liars. Severing started a campaign against the Reich Ministry of War at a secret press conference and I have made an appointment to see him straight after Easter. It's a pity that even this man still can't shake off certain practices which he picked up in his period as a Socialist campaigner. A journalist who attended this conference told us that as regards the Prussian elections Severing has completely lost his head. After the events of the past few days, I am quite glad that a counterweight exists in the shape of the Nazis though they too are naughty boys and must be handled with extreme care. If they did not exist one would really have to invent them. The course which your Excellency is following – no one's friend and no one's enemy – is, I believe, in these circumstances the only correct one. In order to maintain this position above the parties and lay emphasis on it, I have used your authority to turn down all invitations to speak. Everybody knows where you stand as regards the Old Gentleman [Hindenburg], but were you to take an active part in the public election campaign it would create an unfortunate precedent ...

Schleicher letter to Groener, 23 March 1932, in J. Noakes and G. Pridham, eds, *Documents on Nazism 1919–1945*, Jonathan Cape, London, 1974, p. 128.

DOCUMENT 19   STRESEMANN'S SPEECH TO THE
                EXECUTIVE COMMITTEE OF THE DVP,
                26 FEBRUARY 1928

Stresemann's career in the Weimar Republic was devoted not only to the conduct of foreign relations but to the development of responsible parliamentary traditions in Germany. Both activities required a constant and exhausting expenditure of energy on Stresemann's part to convince his colleagues in the DVP of the validity of his views.

Let us not fool ourselves about this: we are in the midst of a parliamentary crisis that is already more than a crisis of conscience. This crisis has two roots: one the caricature that has become of the parliamentary system in Germany, secondly the completely false position of parliament in relation to its responsibility to the nation.

What does 'parliamentary system' mean? It means the responsibility of the Reich minister to parliament, which can pass a vote of no confidence and force him to resign. In no way does it entail the allocation of ministerial offices according to the strength of the parliamentary parties. In no way does it entail the transference of government from the cabinet to the parliamentary parties. The minister is designated by the Reich President. It is clear that the President must take into account that ministers named by him secure the support of the majority of the Reichstag. Moreover, the appointment and dismissal of ministers is a question of their personal responsibility. I personally guard against the adoption of the idea that a parliamentary party 'withdraws' its minister. The ministers have to ask themselves whether they will accept office or give it up. The Reichstag can withdraw its confidence from them. The parliamentary party can exclude them from its membership, but 'withdrawing' a minister means in reality that the individual ceases to exist and becomes a mere agent of one or another organisation. This conception means the end of liberalism in general. When we no longer have any liberal parties who can put up with the individual then they will cease to be bearers of liberalism.

H. Michaelis, E. Schraepler, G. Scheel, eds, *Ursachen und Folgen. Vom deutschen Zusammenbruch 1918 und 1945 bis zur staatlichen Neuordnung Deutschlands in der Gegenwart*, Dokumentation-Verlag, Berlin, 1958, vol. 7, pp. 236–7.

DOCUMENT 20   MÜLLER'S TALK WITH PARTY LEADERS, 11 DECEMBER 1929

Throughout the Republic's history, laborious discussions were needed to secure working agreement between the different parties proposing to form a coalition. Not only did this horse-trading bring the parliamentary process into general disrespect, but it also threatened to paralyse governments during periods of crisis. The following passage graphically illustrates the difficulties of the Müller government in tackling the economic crisis in Germany after 1928.

Present: Müller, Curtius, Hilferding, Moldenhauer, Wissell, v. Guerard, Schätzel, Stegerwald, Dietrich, Wirth; StS Pünder, Popitz, Trendelenburg; MinDir von Hagenow, Schwerin, v. Krosigk, Zarden, Zechlin; *from the parties* : for the SPD: Breitscheid, Wels, Dittman, Hertz; *for the Centre* :

Brüning, Ersing; *for the DVP* : Zapf, Hoff; *for the DDP* : Haas, Fischer; *for the BVP*: Leicht, Horlacher.

(Finance Programme)

The Reich Chancellor called upon the party spokesmen to make known the views of the parties on the government's financial programme.

Deputy *Breitscheid* replied that the discussions of his party were not yet finished. He could, however, already say that his party would indeed participate in the emergency measures but that a commitment to the fourteen individual points of the financial programme did not seem possible. The Social Democracy urgently wanted a crisis to be avoided; they were thus prepared to support the government in the further working out of the financial programme.

Deputy *Zapf* declared that his party could not yet decide to promise their support to the government for the financial programme in its present form. The party strongly distrusted the division of the whole project into immediate measures and a final programme. To agree to the emergency measures without binding guarantees of the final programme being carried out was an impossibility for his party.

Deputy *Brüning* declared that his party could declare itself broadly in agreement with the financial programme, providing the other government parties gave it their approval.

Deputy *Haas* said that the discussions of his party were not yet finished. He hoped, however, that it would be possible to at least come to an agreement on specific points after further debate.

Deputy *Leicht* said that his party completely supported the emergency measures, that they were also ready to give the government a vote of confidence for the foreign policy negotiations at the Hague Conference, but that it was impossible for them to agree to the fourteen points of the whole programme.

The Reich Chancellor concluded on the basis of these remarks that as yet he had not succeeded in getting the parties behind the government. The Reich government nonetheless held firm to its programme and still demanded its complete acceptance by the parties.

Since the further discussion produced no more agreement on the disputed issues, the Reich Chancellor declared that the Cabinet would come to a decision over the situation which had been created by the stand of the parties. He left the party leaders in no doubt, however, that in all probability the decision of the government would be to put the finance programme before the Reichstag, in spite of the negative stand of the parties, in order to achieve a decision in open pitched battle.

Das Kabinett Müller II, Akten der Reichskanzlei, Weimarer Republik, Harald Boldt Verlag, Boppard am Rhein, 1970, vol. 2, pp. 1246–7.

DOCUMENT 21 BRÜNING ON PERSONALITIES

As Hermann Müller's 'Great Coalition' struggled without success to tackle the mounting economic and political crisis in Germany after 1928, the Reichswehr *leaders began to prepare the ground for the emergence of a new government, which would be based on the more moderate rightist groups in Germany, in order to forestall further successes by the extreme rightist elements. An ideal candidate to head the proposed government, which would be equipped with emergency powers, was Heinrich Brüning, of the Centre Party. The following account gives a revealing and disturbing insight into the system of government in the last years of the Weimar Republic.*

A few days later Treviranus came to visit me and said that it was time things were made clear; Groener wanted to discuss the political situation with me. I gave him to understand that all these exchanges were premature and that things could hold out with Hermann Müller until the autumn of 1930. In any case, on grounds of loyalty alone, I could not be the successor of Herman Müller. I would be quite ready to make this clear myself to Groener. ... I was told that we should meet together on the second evening of Christmas at the Willisens. On this evening, to my astonishment, there were at the Willisens not only Groener and Treviranus but also Schleicher, State Secretary Meissner and Ministerial Director Brandenburg. After the meal, Schleicher and Meissner began to make it clear to me that the Reich President was in no way inclined to leave in office the Müller Cabinet once the Young Plan was settled and that he expected me not to ignore his pleas.

I set out the reasons why I believed that the Müller Cabinet must remain in office under all circumstances until late autumn. Meissner countered by explaining that I would not succeed in convincing the President of my view. Hermann Müller would be toppled and his successor would get powers under Article 48 in the event of emergency. I made the same representations as I had eight months earlier to Schleicher and pointed out that in the summer of 1929 a talk had taken place on my initiative between Hugenberg and Kaas with the purpose of establishing Hugenberg's readiness to form a government with the Centre in the autumn of 1930 in the event of the collapse of the Müller Cabinet.

Hugenberg expressed his agreement, yet one must consider that it would be very difficult for Hugenberg to enter a government immediately after the acceptance of the Young Plan. Quite apart from the fact that the French would surely make difficulties for such a cabinet over the evacuation of the Rhineland. In any case, I considered it politically wrong to deprive Hermann Müller of the fruits of the acceptance of the Young Plan, namely the evacuation of the Rhineland, and burden him only with unpleasant things. That would cause later on an exceptional bitterness, the Left would create an uproar against the vital and far reaching financial and social reforms that were needed, with the result that, as in 1925 and 1927, a cabinet of the Right would again collapse and parliament would again come under the sway of a social democracy that had been once more estranged from *Realpolitik*.

Groener, Schleicher and Meissner replied by stating that there was no question of an appointment for Hugenberg, even in the autumn, the President did not want this man. Consequently, one had to prepare in any case for a difficult situation, which the President foresaw yet did not want to shirk. Groener made admiring remarks about the character and decision of the President which, coming from him, were especially significant for me.

I said that I would never avoid an unpleasant duty, if I had no desire in the normal course of events to be a minister. I had to reaffirm at the same time that the earliest suitable moment for a change of government could only be after the Rhineland evacuation. The mood became cool. I could see that Brandenburg above all was put out by my comments. Groener, Meissner and Willisen remained seated with me. Frau von Willisen went with Schleicher and Treviranus into the next room. There Schleicher told Treviranus: 'So, you see, Brüning won't do it so there's nothing else but for me to do it.'

Groener tried to make it plain to me that he had decisive influence over the old Gentleman (Hindenburg) and that he knew that the President would stand behind me to the last. He asked me to think over the matter again and to go out with him alone one Sunday to talk things over calmly. I expressed my readiness to do this but could not change my opinion.

Brüning's account of the talk, in his *Memoiren 1918–1934*, Deutsche Verlags-Anstalt, Stuttgart, 1970, pp. 150–2.

DOCUMENT 22   GOEBBELS ADDRESSES THE REICHSTAG ON 5 FEBRUARY 1931

Some idea of what the NSDAP meant by the 'legal' road to power was given in the following speech by the Gauleiter of Berlin, Goebbels. It is one of many examples where the party spokesman made quite clear what could be expected from a Hitler government. In the light of such utterances one must assume that the conservative elites who expected to 'contain' Hitler were being at best wildly optimistic. There are less charitable conclusions to be drawn.

The more the Government believes itself to be firmly in control, the more watchful is the Opposition. On 14 September it broke through for the first time to the German public too. Since 14 September we have again set waves of agitation in motion. If today we did no more, national socialism would grow, because the Government is working for national socialism. What you, Mr Reich Chancellor, lose in support, we gain. The national socialist movement has no intention of abandoning its defiant opposition to the present regime. The national socialist movement continues unwaveringly to oppose this system.

[The movement] has declared, in the words of its leader, that it is legal. That signifies, however, that with respect to the constitution we are committed only to the legality of its ways, but not to the legality of its ends. We wish to gain power legally. But how we use that power when we get it, that is our concern. We have the feeling that the German people intend, sooner or later, to demand a reckoning with the sort of politics conducted in Germany since 1918. If the nation demands this reckoning, and if the nation appoints us the executor of its will, then, true to the principle that the will of the people is the supreme law, we shall not shirk our duty.

Printed in E. Deuerlein, ed., *Der Aufstieg der NSDAP in Augenzeugenberichten*, 3rd edition, Deutscher Taschenbuch Verlag, Munich, 1978, pp. 347–8.

DOCUMENT 23   **THE ELECTIONS OF SUMMER 1932**

The following passage brings out the growing mood of despair among responsible commentators on the political scene in Germany after the fall of Heinrich Brüning in 1930. The depressing conclusions were drawn after a long run of success at the polls by the NSDAP.

Looked at politically, objectively, the result of the election is so fearful because it seems clear that the present election will be the last normal Reichstag election for a long time to come. The so-called race of thinkers and poets is hurrying with flags flying towards dictatorship and thus towards a period that will be filled with severe revolutionary disturbances. The elected Reichstag is totally incapable of functioning, even if the Centre goes in with the National Socialists, which it will do without hesitation if it seems in the interests of the party. Genuine bourgeois parties no long exist. The bourgeoisie has excluded itself as a factor in the political process and will probably have to pay dearly for it.

The one consolation could be the recognition that the National Socialists have passed their peak, since, in comparison with the Prussian elections, they have declined in most constituencies, but against this stands the fact that the radicalism of the right has unleashed a strong radicalism on the left. The communists have made gains almost everywhere and thus internal political disturbances have become exceptionally bitter. If things are faced squarely and soberly the situation is such that much more than half the German people have declared themselves against the present state, but have not said what sort of state they would accept. Thus any organic development is for the moment impossible. As the lesser of many evils to be feared, I think, would be the open assumption of dictatorship by the present government. ...

Extract from a memorandum by Reich Minister of the Interior Dr Külz, in H. Michaelis et al., eds, *Ursachen und Folgen*, vol. 7, pp. 324–5.

BIBLIOGRAPHY

The bibliography has been thoroughly revised and extended to take account of new work since the first edition of this book. Readers familiar with the history of the Weimar Republic will recognise at once the debt owed to works in the German language. The requirements of the series preclude listing these at any length. Those few German volumes which are included in the bibliography are those to which I have directly referred in the main text.

GENERAL ACCOUNTS

1   Abraham, D., *The Collapse of the Weimar Republic*, 2nd edn, Holmes & Meier, New York, London, 1986.
2   Bessel, R., Feuchtwanger, E.J., ed., *Social Change and Political Development in Weimar Germany*, Croom Helm, London, 1981.
3   Bracher, K.D., *Die Auflösung der Weimarer Republik. Eine Studie zum Problem des Machtverfalls in der Demokratie*, 4th edn, Ring-Verlag, Schwarzwald, 1964.
4   Breuilly, J., ed., *The State of Germany: The National Idea in the Making, Unmaking and Remaking of a Modern Nation-State*, Longman, London, 1992.
5   Broszat, M., *Hitler and the Collapse of Weimar Germany*, Berg, Oxford, 1987.
6   Bullivant, K., ed., *Culture and Society in the Weimar Republic*, Manchester University Press, Manchester, 1977.
7   Carsten, F.L., *Essays in German History*, Hambledon Press, London, 1985.
8   Castellan, G., *L'Allemagne de Weimar 1918–1933*, Libraire Armand Colin, Paris, 1969.
9   Chickering, R.P., 'The Reichsbanner and the Weimar Republic 1924–1926', *Journal of Modern History*, xl, no. 4, 1968, 524–34.
10 Craig, G.A., 'Engagement and neutrality in Weimar Germany', *Journal of Contemporary History*, vi, no. 4, 1971, 3–28.
11 Craig, G., *Germany 1866–1945*, Clarendon Press, Oxford, 1978.
12 Dorpalen, A., *Hindenburg and the Weimar Republic*, Princeton University Press, Princeton, NJ, 1964.

13　Eksteins, M., *The Limits of Reason. The German Democratic Press and the Collapse of Weimar Democracy*, Oxford University Press, Oxford, 1975.

14　Epstein, K., *Matthias Erzberger and the Dilemma of German Democracy*, Princeton University Press, Princeton, NJ, 1959.

15　Erdman, K.D., Schulze, H., eds, *Weimar: Selbstpreisgabe einer Demokratie. Eine Bilanz Heute*, Droste, Düsseldorf, 1980.

16　Evans, R.J., *The Feminist Movement in Germany 1894–1933*, Sage, London, 1976.

17　Eyck, E., *A History of the Weimar Republic*, 2 vols, paperback edn, J. Wiley, New York, 1967.

18　Feuchtwanger, E.J., *Prussia: Myth and Reality*, Oswald Wolff, London, 1970.

19　Feuchtwanger, E.J., *From Weimar to Hitler*, Macmillan, London, 1993.

20　Fromm, E., *The Working Class in Weimar Germany. A Psychological and Sociological Study*, Berg, Oxford, 1984.

21　Gay, P., *Weimar Culture. The Outsider as Insider*, Secker & Warburg, London, 1969.

22　Gooch, G.P., *Germany*, Benn, London, 1926.

23　Holborn, H., *A History of Modern Germany 1840–1945*, Eyre & Spottiswoode, London, 1969.

24　Hughes, M., *Nationalism and Society. Germany 1800–1945*, Edward Arnold, London, 1988.

25　Koch, H.W., *A History of Prussia*, Longman, London, 1974.

26　Kolb, E., *The Weimar Republic*, Unwin Hyman, London, 1988.

27　Lebovics, H., *Social Conservatism and the Middle Classes in Germany 1914–1933*, Princeton University Press, Princeton, NJ, 1969.

28　Maier, C., *Recasting Bourgeois Europe: Germany and Italy in the Period after World War I*, Princeton University Press, Princeton, NJ, 1975.

29　Mann, G., *The History of Germany since 1789*, Chatto & Windus, London, 1968.

30　Meinecke, F., *The German Catastrophe*, Beacon Press, Boston, MA, 1963.

31　Nicholls, A.J. and Mathias, E., eds, *German Democracy and the Triumph of Hitler. Essays in Recent German History*, Allen & Unwin, London, 1971.

32　Ringer, F.K., *The Decline and Fall of the German Mandarins. The German Academic Community 1890–1933*, Harvard University Press, Cambridge, MA, 1969.

33　Rosenberg, A., *A History of the German Republic*, Methuen, London, 1936.

34　Stachura, P.D., *The German Youth Movement 1900–1945. An Interpretative and Documentary History*, Macmillan, London, 1981.

35   Stachura, P.D., *The Weimar Era and Hitler, 1918–1933. A Critical Bibliography*, Clio, Oxford, 1978.
36   Stern, F., *The Failure of Illiberalism. Essays on the Political Culture of Modern Germany*, Knopf, New York, 1972.
37   Willett, J., *Art and Politics in the Weimar period 1917–1933*, Thames & Hudson, London, 1978.
38   Williamson, J.G., *Karl Helfferich 1872–1924*, Princeton University Press, Princeton, NJ, 1972.
39   Winkler, H.A., *Weimar 1918–1933. Die Geschichte der ersten deutschen Demokratie*, Beck Verlag, Munich, 1993.

CONSTITUTION/REVOLUTION

40   Burdick, C.B. and Lutz, R.H., *The Political Institutions of the German Revolution*, Praeger, New York, 1966.
41   Buse, D.K., 'Ebert and the German crisis 1917–1920', *Central European History*, v, no. 3, 1972, 234–55.
42   Caplan, J., *Government Without Administration. State and Civil Service in Weimar and Nazi Germany*, Clarendon Press, Oxford, 1989.
43   Carsten, F.L., *Revolution in Central Europe 1918–1919*, Temple Smith, London, 1972.
44   Feldman, G.D., *Army, Industry and Labour in Germany 1914–1918*, Princeton University Press, Princeton, NJ, 1966.
45   Glees, A., 'Albert C. Grzesinski and the politics of Prussia, 1926–30', *English Historical Review*, 353, 1974, 814–34.
46   Herwig, H., 'The first German Congress of Workers' and Soldiers' councils and the problem of military reform', *Central European History*, i, no. 2, 1968, 150ff.
47   Hunt, R.N., 'Friedrich Ebert and the German Revolution of 1918' in L. Krieger and F. Stern, eds, *The Responsibility of Power. Historical Essays in honour of H. Holborn*, Macmillan, London, 1938, 315–34.
48   Kitchen, M., *The Silent Dictatorship. The Politics of the German High Command under Hindenburg and Ludendorff*, Croom Helm, London, 1977.
49   Koch, H.W., *A Constitutional History of Germany in the Nineteenth and Twentieth Centuries*, Longman, London, 1984.
50   Koehler, E.D., 'Revolutionary Pomerania 1919–1920. A study in majority socialist agricultural policy and civil-military relations', *Central European History*, ix, no. 3, 1976, 250–93.
51   König, F., ed., *Friedrich Ebert und seine Zeit. Bilanz und Perspektiven*, 2nd edn, Oldenbourg Verlag, Munich, 1991.
52   Kunz, A., *Civil Servants and the Politics of Inflation in Germany 1914–1924*, Walter de Gruyter, Berlin–New York, 1986.

53   Mitchell, A., *Revolution in Bavaria 1918–1919. The Eisner Regime and the Soviet Republic*, Princeton University Press, Princeton, NJ, 1965.

54   Pryce, D.B., 'The Reich Government and Saxony 1923', *Central European History*, x, no. 2, 1977, 112–47.

55   Rürup, R., 'Problems of the German Revolution 1918–1919', *Journal of Contemporary History*, iii, no. 4, 1968, 109–35.

56   Ryder, A.J., *The German Revolution of 1918. A Study of German Socialism in War and Revolt*, Cambridge University Press, Cambridge, MA, 1967.

57   Tampke, J., *The Ruhr and Revolution. The Revolutionary Movement in the Rhenish-Westphalian Region*, Croom Helm, London, 1979.

58   Tracy, D.R., 'Reform in the early Weimar Republic. The Thuringian example', *Journal of Modern History*, xliv, no. 2, 1972, 195–212.

VERSAILLES/FOREIGN POLICY

59   Adamthwaite, A., *The Lost Peace 1918–1939. International Relations in Europe*, Edward Arnold, London, 1980.

60   Bell, P.M.H., *The Origins of the Second World War in Europe*, Longman, London, 1986.

61   Bretton, H.L., *Stresemann and the Revision of Versailles*, Stanford University Press, Stanford, CA, 1953.

62   Carsten, F.L., *Britain and the Weimar Republic. The British Documents*, Batsford, London, 1984.

63   Cienciala, A.M. and Komarnicki,T., *From Versailles to Locarno. Keys to Polish Foreign Policy*, Kansas University Press, Lawrence, KS, 1984.

64   Cornebise, A.E., 'Gustav Stresemann and the Ruhr occupation. The making of a Statesman', *European Studies Review*, ii, no. 1, 1972, 43–67.

65   Crampton, R., *Eastern Europe in the Twentieth Century*, Routledge, London, 1994.

66   Duroselle, J.B., 'The spirit of Locarno: Illusions of pactomania', *Foreign Affairs*, 50, 1971, 752–64.

67   Dyck, H.L., *Weimar Germany and Soviet Russia 1926–1933. A Study in Diplomatic Instability*, Chatto & Windus, London, 1966.

68   Enssle, M., *Stresemann's Territorial Revisionism: Germany, Belgium and the Eupen Malmedy Question 1919–1929*, Weisbaden, Mainz, 1979.

69   Fink, C., 'Defender of minorities. Germany in the League of Nations 1926–33', *Central European History*, v, 1972, 330–57.

70   Fink, C., 'Stresemann's minority policies 1934–1929', *Journal of Contemporary History*, xiv, 1979, 403–22.

71   Fink, C., *The Genoa Conference. European Diplomacy 1921–1922*, University of North Carolina Press, Chapel Hill, NC, 1984.

72   Freund, G., *Unholy Alliance*, Chatto & Windus, London, 1966.
73   Grathwol, R., 'Gustav Stresemann. Reflections on his foreign policy', *Journal of Modern History*, 45, no. 1, 1973, 52–70.
74   Grathwol, R., 'Stresemann revisited', *European Studies Review*, vii, 1977, 341–52.
75   Grathwol, R., *Stresemann and the DNVP. Reconciliation or Revenge in German Foreign Policy 1924–1928*, Regents Press, Lawrence, KS, 1980.
76   Grathwol, R.P., 'Germany and the Eupen-Malmedy affair 1924–26. Here lies the spirit of Locarno', *Central European History*, viii, 1975, 221–50.
77   Gromada, T. von, *Essays on Poland's Foreign Policy 1918–1939*, Joseph Pilsudski Institute, New York, 1970.
78   Henig, R., *Versailles and After*, Methuen, London, 1984.
79   Hiden, J.W., *Germany and Europe 1919–1939*, 2nd edn, Longman, London, 1993.
80   Hiden, J.W., *The Baltic States and Weimar Ostpolitik*, Cambridge University Press, Cambridge, 1977.
81   Hiden, J.W., 'The Weimar Republic and the problem of the *Auslandsdeutsche*', *Journal of Contemporary History*, xii, 1977, 273–89.
82   Hildebrand, K., *German Foreign Policy from Bismarck to Adenauer. The limits of Statecraft*, Hyman, London, 1989.
83   Himmer, R., 'Soviet policy towards Germany during the Russo-Polish war', *Slavic Review*, 35, no. 4, 1976, 665–82.
84   Jacobsen, J., *Locarno Diplomacy*, Princeton University Press, Princeton, NJ, 1972.
85   Jaffe, L.S., *The Decision to Disarm Germany. British Policy towards Postwar German Disarmament, 1914–1919*, Allen & Unwin, London, 1985.
86   Joll, J., 'The foundations of German foreign policy', *History*, 62, no. 205, 1977, 253–8.
87   Jones, K.P., 'Stresemann, the Ruhr crisis and Rhenish separatism. A case study of Westpolitik', *European Studies Review*, vii, 1977, 311–40.
88   Kimmich, C.M., ed., *German Foreign Policy 1918–1945*, Scholarly Resources Inc., Wilmington, DE, 1981.
89   Kimmich, C.M., *The Free City. Danzig and German Foreign Policy 1918–1934*, Yale University Press, New Haven, CT, 1968.
90   Kochan, L., *Russia and the Weimar Republic*, Bowes & Bowes, Cambridge, 1954.
91   Kollman, E.C., 'Walther Rathenau and German foreign policy. Thoughts and actions', *Journal of Modern History*, xiv, 1952, 127–42.
92   Krüger, P., *Die Aussenpolitik der Republik von Weimar*, Wissenschaftliche Buchgesellschaft Darmstadt, 1985.

93   Laqueur, W., *Russia and Germany. A Century of Conflict*,
      Weidenfeld & Nicolson, London, 1965.
94   Lee, M., Michalka, W., *German Foreign Policy 1917–1933.
      Continuity or Break?*, Berg, Leamington Spa, 1987.
95   Low, A.D., *The Anschluss Movement 1918–1919 and the Paris
      Peace Conference*, Philadelphia, PA, 1974.
96   Lundgreen-Nielson, K., *The Polish Problem at the Paris Peace
      Conference. A Study of the Politics of the Great Powers and the
      Poles, 1918–1919*, Odense University Press, Odense, 1979.
97   Martel, G., ed., *The Origins of the Second World War Reconsidered.
      The A.J.P. Taylor Debate after Twenty-Five Years*, Allen & Unwin,
      London, 1986.
98   Mayer, A.J., *Politics and Diplomacy of Peacemaking. Containment
      and Counterrevolution at Versailles, 1918/19*, Weidenfeld &
      Nicolson, London, 1968.
99   Michalka, W. and Lee, M.M., eds, *Gustav Stresemann*, Darmstadt,
      1984.
100   Moore, S., *Peace Without Victory for the Allies, 1918–1932*, Berg,
      Oxford–Washington, DC, 1994.
101   Nelson, H.I., *Land and Power. British and Allied Policy on
      Germany's Frontiers 1916–19*, Routledge & Kegan Paul, London,
      1968.
102   Orde, A., *British Policy and European Reconstruction after the First
      World War*, Cambridge University Press, Cambridge, 1990.
103   Post, G. Jr, *The Civil-Military Fabric of Weimar Foreign Policy*,
      Princeton University Press, Princeton, NJ, 1973.
104   Ratliff, W., *Faithful to the Fatherland. Julius Curtius and Weimar
      Foreign Policy*, Peter Lang, New York, 1990.
105   Riekhof, H. von, *German–Polish Relations 1918–1933*, Johns
      Hopkins University Press, Baltimore, MD, 1971.
106   Rosenthal, H.K., *German and Pole. National Conflict and Modern
      Myth*, University Press of Florida, Gainesville, FL, 1976.
107   Schulz, G., *Revolutions and Peace Treaties*, Methuen, London, 1971.
108   Stirk, P., ed., *Mitteleuropa. History and Prospects*, Edinburgh
      University Press, Edinburgh, 1994.
109   Suval, S., *The Anschluss Question in the Weimar Era. A Study of
      Nationalism in Germany and Austria*, Johns Hopkins University
      Press, Baltimore–London, 1974.
110   Urban, L.K., 'German property interests in Poland during the 1920s',
      East European Quarterly, 10, 1976, 181–221.
111   Williamson, D.G., *The British in Germany 1918–1930. The
      Reluctant Occupiers*, Berg, Oxford–London, 1991.

PARTIES/COALITION POLITICS

112 Breitman, R., *German Socialism and Weimar Democracy*, University of North Carolina Press, Chapel Hill, NC, 1981.

113 Cary, N.D., 'The making of the Reich President 1925: German conservatism and the nomination of Paul von Hindenburg', *Central European History*, xxiii, no. 2/3, 1990, 179–204.

114 Evans, E.L., *The German Centre Party 1870–1933*, Illinois University Press, Illinois, IL, 1981.

115 Falter, J.W., 'The two Hindenburg Elections of 1925 and 1932', *Central European History*, xxiii, no. 2/3, 1990, 225–41.

116 Frye, B.B., *Liberal Democrats in the Weimar Republic. The History of the German Democratic Party and the German State Party*, Southern Illinois University Press, Carbondale, Edwardsville, Illinois, 1985.

117 Gates, R.A., 'German socialism and the crisis of 1929–1933', *Central European History*, vii, no. 4, 1974, 232–59.

118 Glees, A., 'Albert C. Grzesinski and the politics of Prussia, 1926–30', *English Historical Review*, 353, 1974, 814–34.

119 Guttsman, W.L., *Workers' Culture in Weimar Germany. Between Tradition and Commitment*, Berg, Oxford–Washington, 1990.

120 Guttsman, W.L., *The German Social Democratic Party, 1875–1933*, Allen & Unwin, London, 1981.

121 Hunt, J.C., 'The bourgeois middle in German politics 1871–1933', *Central European History*, xi, no. 1, 1978, 83ff.

122 Hunt, R.N., *German Social Democracy 1918–1933*, Yale University Press, New Haven, CT, 1964.

123 Jarausch, K.H. and Jones, L.E., eds, *In Search of a Liberal Germany*, Berg, New York–Oxford, 1990.

124 Jones, L.E., *German Liberalism and the Dissolution of the Weimar Party System 1918–1933*, Chapel Hill, London, 1988.

125 Jones, L.E., *Between Reform and Resistance. Studies in the History of German Conservatism from 1789 to 1945*, Berg, Oxford–Washington, 1993.

126 Jones, L.E., 'Gustav Stresemann and the crisis of German Liberalism', *European Studies Review*, iv, no. 2, 1974, 141–63.

127 Jones, L.E., 'The dying middle. Weimar Germany and the fragmentation of Bourgeois politics', *Central European History*, v, 1972, 23–54.

128 Knapp, T.A., 'The Red and the Black. Catholic socialists in the Weimar Republic', *Catholic History Review*, 61, no. 3, 1975, 386–408.

129 Laubach, E., *Die Politik der Kabinette Wirth 1921–1922*, Matthieson Verlag, Lübeck–Hamburg, 1968.

130 Miller, S. and Potthof, H., *A History of the SPD from 1848 to the Present*, Berg, Oxford, 1986.

131   Neumann, S., *Die Parteien der Weimarer Republik*, paperback reprint, W. Kohlhammer, Stuttgart, 1965.
132   Ruppert, K., *Im Dienst der Staat von Weimar. Das Zentrum als regierende Partei in der Weimarer Republik*, Droste, Düsseldorf, 1992.
133   Stürmer, M., *Koalition und Opposition in der Weimarer Republik 1924–1928*, Droste, Düsseldorf, 1967.
134   Turner, H.A., *Stresemann and the Politics of the Weimar Republic*, Princeton University Press, Princeton, NJ, 1963.

ECONOMICS/REPARATIONS

135   Barclay, D.E., 'Wichard von Moellendorff and the dilemmas of economic planning in Germany 1918/19', *Central European History*, xi, no. 1, 1978, 50ff.
136   Bennett, E.W., *Germany and the Diplomacy of the Financial Crisis*, Harvard University Press, Cambridge, MA, 1962.
137   Boehme, H., *An Introduction to the Social and Economic History of Germany*, Blackwell, London, 1979.
138   Bravo, G.F., 'In the name of our mutual friend. The Keynes–Cuno affair', *Journal of Contemporary History*, xxiv, no.1, 1989, 147–68.
139   Bry, G., *Wages in Germany 1871–1945*, Princeton University Press, Princeton, NJ, 1960.
140   Evans, R.J. and Geary, D., *The German Unemployed 1918–1936*, Croom Helm, London, 1987.
141   Falkus, M., 'The German business cycle in the 1920s', *Economic History Review*, xxiii, 1975, pp. 451–65.
142   Feldman, G.D., 'Industrialists, bankers and the problem of unemployment in the Weimar Republic', *Central European History*, xxv, no. 1, 1993, 76–96.
143   Felix, D., *Walther Rathenau and the Weimar Republic. The Politics of Reparations*, Johns Hopkins University Press, Baltimore, MD, 1971.
144   Guttmann,W. and Meehan, P., *The Great Inflation 1923*, Saxon House, Farnborough, 1975.
145   James, H., *The German Slump. Politics and Economics 1924–1936*, Clarendon Press, Oxford, 1984.
146   Kent, B., *The Spoils of War. The Politics, Economics and Diplomacy of Reparations 1918–1932*, Clarendon Press, Oxford, 1989.
147   Kruedener, J. von, ed., *Economic Crisis and Political Collapse: The Weimar Republic 1924–33*, Berg, Oxford, 1988.
148   Nicholls, A.J., *Freedom with Responsibility. The Social Market Economy in Germany 1918–1963*, Clarendon Press, Oxford, 1993.
149   Overy, R.J., *The Nazi Economic Recovery 1932–1938*, Macmillan, London, 1982.

150 Ringer, F.K., *The German Inflation of 1923*, Oxford University Press, Oxford, 1969.
151 Rowley, E.E., *Hyperinflation in Germany*, Scolar Press, Aldershot, 1994.
152 Rupieper, H.J., *The Cuno Government and Reparations 1922–1923*, Nijhoff, The Hague, 1979.
153 Schuker, S.A., *The End of French Predominance in Europe. The Financial Crisis of 1924 and the Adoption of the Dawes Plan*, University of North Carolina Press, Chapel Hill, NC, 1976.
154 Stachura, P.D., ed., *Unemployment and the Great Depression in Weimar Germany*, Macmillan, London, 1987.
155 Stolper, G., *The German Economy 1870 to the Present*, Weidenfeld & Nicolson, London, 1967.
156 Trachtenberg, M., *Reparations in World Politics*, Columbia University Press, New York, 1980.
157 Williamson, D., 'Walther Rathenau. Realist, pedagogue, prophet', *European Studies Review*, vi, 1976, 99–121.
158 Williamson, D., 'Walther Rathenau: patron saint of the German liberal establishment', *Leo Baeck Institute Year Book*, vol. 20, 1975, 207–22.

LEFTIST OPPOSITION

159 Badia, G., 'La place de Rosa Luxemburg dans le mouvement socialiste', *Revue Historique*, 511, 1974, 107–18.
160 Bassler, G.P., 'The communist movement in the German revolution 1918–19. A problem of historical typology?', *Central European History*, vi, 1973, 233–77.
161 Fischer, C., *The German Communists and the Rise of Nazism*, Macmillan, London, 1991.
162 Castellan, G., 'A propos de Rosa Luxemburg', *Revue Historique*, xxiii, 1982, 573–82.
163 Comfort, R.A., *Revolutionary Hamburg Labour Politics in the Early Weimar Republic*, Stanford University Press, Stanford, CA, 1966.
164 Deak, I., *A Political History of the Weltbuehne and its Circle*, University of California Press, Berkeley, CA, 1969.
165 Fowkes, B., *Communism in Germany under the Weimar Republic*, Macmillan, London, 1984.
166 Krause, H., *USPD, Zur Geschichte der Unabhängige Sozialdemokratishen Partei*, Frankfurt, Europäische Verlaganstalt, Frankfurt–Cologne, 1975.
167 Levine-Meyer, R., *Inside German Communism. Memoirs of Party Life in the Weimar Republic*, Pluto Press, London, 1977.
168 Morgan, D., *The Socialist Left and the German Revolution. A History of the German Independent Social Democratic Party 1917–1922*, Cornell University Press, Ithaca, NY, 1976.

169 Nettl, J.P., *Rosa Luxemburg*, 2 vols, Oxford University Press, Oxford, 1966.
170 Rosenhaft, E., *Beating the Fascists? The German Communists and the Rise of Nazism*, Cambridge University Press, Cambridge, 1983.

RIGHTIST OPPOSITION

171 Allen, W.S., *The Nazi Seizure of Power: The Experience of a Single German Town*, 2nd edn, Eyre & Spottiswoode, London, 1995.
172 Broszat, M., *The Hitler State*, Longman, London, 1981.
173 Bullock, A., *Hitler. A Study in Tyranny*, Odhams Press, London, 1960.
174 Carr, W., *Hitler. A Study in Personality and Politics*, Edward Arnold, London, 1978.
175 Carsten, F.L., *The Rise of Fascism*, Batsford, London, 1967.
176 Carsten, F.L., *Fascist Movements in Austria. From Schoener to Hitler*, Sage, London, 1977.
177 Chamberlin, B.S., *The Enemy on the Right. The Alldeutsch Verband in the Weimar Republic*, Ann Arbor, MI, 1973.
178 Chanady, A., 'The disintegration of the German National People's Party, 1924–1930', *Journal of Modern History*, xxxix, 1967, 65–91.
179 Childers, T., *The Nazi Voter. The Social Foundations of Fascism in Germany, 1919–1933*, University of North Carolina Press, Chapel Hill, NC, 1983.
180 Elliott, C.J., *Rehearsals for Fascism. Populism and Political Mobilisation in Weimar Germany*, Oxford University Press, Oxford, 1990.
181 Faris, E., 'Takeoff point for the National Socialist Party. The Landtag election in Baden 1929', *Central European History*, viii, no. 2, 1975, 140–71.
182 Farquharson, J., 'The NSDAP in Hannover and Lower Saxony 1921–1926', *Journal of Contemporary History*, viii, no. 4, 1973, 103–40.
183 Fest, J., *Hitler*, Weidenfeld & Nicolson, London, 1974.
184 Fischer, C., *Stormtroopers. A Social, Economic and Ideological Analysis 1929–35*, George Allen & Unwin, London, 1983.
185 Gordon, S., *Hitler, Germans and the 'Jewish Question'*, Princeton University Press, Princeton, NJ, 1984.
186 Hamilton, R.F., *Who Voted for Hitler?*, Princeton University Press, Princeton, NJ, 1982.
187 Hayes, P., 'Fritz Roessler and Nazism. The observations of a German industrialist 1930–7', *Central European History*, xx, no. 1, 1987, 58–79.
188 Hertzmann, L., *DNVP-Right-wing Opposition in the Weimar Republic*, Nebraska University Press, Lincoln, NB, 1963.

189 Hitler, A., *Mein Kampf*, trans. R. Mannheim, Hutchinson, London, 1969.
190 Hitler, A., *The Speeches of Adolf Hitler April 1922 to August 1939*, edited by N.H. Baynes, Oxford University Press, Oxford, 1942.
191 Jäckel, E., *Hitler's World View*, Harvard University Press, Cambridge, MA, 1981.
192 Jones, L.E., 'The greatest stupidity of my life. Alfred Hugenberg and the formation of the Hitler coalition', *Journal of Contemporary History*, xxvii, no. 1, 1992, 63–87.
193 Kater, M.H., *The Nazi Party. A Social Profile of Members and Leaders 1919–1945*, Blackwell, Oxford, 1983.
194 Kershaw, I., *Hitler*, Longman, London, 1991.
195 Kershaw, I., *The Nazi Dictatorship. Problems and Perspectives of Interpretation*, 3rd edn, Edward Arnold, London, 1993.
196 Koshar, R., *Social Life, Local Politics and Nazism. Marburg 1880–1935*, University of North Carolina Press, Chapel Hill, NC, 1986.
197 Krebs, A., *The Infancy of Nazism. The Memoirs of ex-Gauleiter Albert Krebs 1923–33*, Croom Helm, London, 1976.
198 Leopold, J.A., *Alfred Hugenberg. The Radical Nationalist Campaign against the Weimar Republic*, Yale University Press, New Haven, CT, 1977.
199 Merkl, P., *Political Violence under the Swastika. 581 Early Nazis*, Princeton University Press, Princeton, NJ, 1975.
200 Milfull, J. ed., *The Attractions of Fascism. Social Psychology and Aesthetics of the 'Triumph of the Right'*, Berg, Oxford–Washington, 1990.
201 Mosse, W.E., *International Fascism: New Research and New Methodologies*, Sage, London, 1980.
202 Mosse, G.L., *The Crisis of German Ideology. Intellectual Origins of the Third Reich*, Weidenfeld & Nicolson, London, 1966.
203 Mühlberger, D., ed., *The Social Basis of European Fascist Movements*, Croom Helm, London, 1987.
204 Mühlberger, D., 'The sociology of the NSDAP. The question of working class membership', *Journal of Contemporary History*, xv, no. 3, 1980, 493–512.
205 Mühlberger, D., *Hitler's Followers. Studies in the Sociology of the Nazi Movement*, Routledge, London, 1991.
206 Noakes, J., *The Nazi Party in Lower Saxony, 1921–1933*, Oxford University Press, Oxford, 1971.
207 Noakes, J. and Pridham, G., eds, *Nazism 1919–1945. A Documentary Reader*, 3 vols, University of Exeter, Exeter, 1983–1988.
208 Orlow, D., *The History of the Nazi Party*, Vol. 1: *1919–1933*, David and Charles, Pittsburgh, PA, 1969.
209 Osmond, J., *Rural Protest in the Weimar Republic. The Free Peasantry in the Rhineland and Bavaria*, Macmillan, London, 1993.

210   Pulzer, P.G.S., *The Rise of Political Anti-Semitism in Germany and Austria*, Wiley, New York, 1964.
211   Salmon, E. von, *The Captive. The Story of an Unknown Political Prisoner*, Weidenfeld & Nicolson, London, 1961.
212   Speier, H., *German White Collar Workers and the Rise of Hitler*, Yale University Press, New Haven, CT, 1987.
213   Stachura, P.D., *Nazi Youth in the Weimar Republic*, Clio Press, 1975.
214   Stachura, P.D., ed., *The Nazi Machtergreifung*, Allen & Unwin, London, 1983.
215   Steinberg, M.S., *Sabres and Brown Shirts. The German Student's Path to National Socialism 1918–35*, University of Chicago Press, Chicago, IL, 1977.
216   Stoakes, G., *Hitler and the Quest for World Dominion. Nazi Ideology and Foreign Policy in the 1920s*, Berg, Leamington Spa, 1986.
217   Taylor, S., *Prelude to Genocide. Nazi Ideology and the Struggle for Power*, Duckworth, London, 1985.
218   Turner, H.A. Jr, *German Big Business and the Rise of Hitler*, Oxford University Press, Oxford, 1985.
219   Walker, D.P., *Alfred Hugenberg and the Deutschnationale Volkspartei*, Cambridge University Press, Cambridge, 1976.
220   Winkler, H.A., 'From social protectionism to National Socialism. The German small business movement in comparative perspective', *Journal of Modern History*, xxxxviii, 1976, 1–18.
221   Woolf, S. ed., *Fascism in Europe*, Methuen, London, 1981.

REICHSWEHR

222   Bennett, E.W., *German Rearmament and the West 1932–1933*, Princeton University Press, Princeton, NJ, 1979
223   Bird, K.W., *Weimar, the German Naval Officer Corps and the Rise of National Socialism*, Amsterdam, 1977.
224   Carroll, D.F., 'The role of Kurt von Schleicher in the fall of the Weimar Republic', *International Review of History and Political Science*, ix, no. 4, 1972, 35–60.
225   Carsten, F.L., *Reichswehr und Politik 1918–1933*, Kiepenheuer & Witsch, Cologne, Berlin, 1964.
226   Craig, G.A., *The Politics of the Prussian Army 1640–1945*, Oxford University Press, Oxford, 1955.
227   Deist, W., ed., *The German Military in the Age of Total War*, Berg, Leamington Spa, 1985.
228   Demeter, K., *The German Officer Corps in Society and State 1650–1945*, Weidenfeld & Nicolson, London, 1965.
229   Diehl, J.M., *Paramilitary Politics in Weimar Germany*, Indiana State University Press, Bloomington, IN, 1977.

230 Dupuy, T.N., *A Genius for War. The German Army and General Staff 1807–1945*, London, 1977.

231 Elliott, C.J., 'The Kriegervereine and the Weimar Republic', *Journal of Contemporary History*, x, no. 1, 1975, 109–29.

232 Favez, J.-C., 'Hitler et la Reichswehr en 1923', *Revue d'Histoire Moderne et Contemporaine*, xvii, 1970, 22–49.

233 Goerlitz, W., *History of the German General Staff 1657–1945*, Praeger, New York, 1967.

234 Gordon, H.J., *The Reichswehr and the German Republic 1919–1926*, Princeton University Press, Princeton, NJ, 1957.

235 Hayes, P., 'A question mark with epaulettes? Kurt von Schleicher and Weimar politics', *Journal of Modern History*, lii, no. 1, 1980, 35–65.

236 Müller, K.-J., *The Army, Politics and Society in Germany, 1933–1945. Studies in the Army's Relation to Nazism*, Manchester University Press, Manchester, 1987.

237 Seeckt, H.W., *Thoughts of a Soldier*, London, 1930.

238 Wheeler-Bennett, J.W., *Nemesis of Power. The German Army in Politics 1918–1945*, Macmillan, London, 1961.

INDEX

agriculture, 20, 34, 35, 43, 61, 64, 66, 70
airforce, 57
Allenstein, 12
Allied and Associated Powers, 2, 9, 10, 11, 22, 25, 26, 27, 28, 30, 33, 50, 57, 60, 63
Allied Control Commission, 23
Alsace-Lorraine, 12
Anhalt, 66
Anschluss, 63, 75
anti-militarism, 4
anti-Semitism, 42, 43, 45, 47, 65, 90, 91
Armistice, 10, 14, 23,
army, *See Reichswehr*
article 48, 5, 16, 61, 67, 71
Austria, 63

Baltic states, 25
Barth, Emil, 72
Bauer, Gustav, 52
Bavaria, 7, 46, 55, 66
Belgium, 12, 27, 75, 76
Bell, Hans, 75
Berlin, 4, 25, 28, 29, 44, 51, 65, 69, 83, 98
Berlin, Treaty of (1926), 28
Bernstorff, Count Johann-Heinrich, 76
'black Reichswehr', 54, 55
blockade, 4
Bolsheviks, 2, 25, 36, 39
bolshevism, 23, 69, 70, 91, 93
Brandenburg, 97, 98

Brandler, Heinrich, 38
Braun, Otto, 80, 86
Braunschweig, 66
Breitscheid, Rudolf, 96, 97
Brockdorff-Rantzau, Count Ulrich von, 75, 76
Brüning, Heinrich, 60, 61, 62, 63, 65, 67, 68, 86, 96, 97–8, 99
Bundesrat, 6, 7
bureaucracy, 3, 7, 20, 42, 67
BVP (Bavarian People's Party), 16, 58, 95

Centre Party, 5, 9, 15, 16, 17, 18, 19, 20, 21, 22, 58, 60, 66, 77, 95
Church, 16, 42, 58, 74
Comintern, 37, 38, 39, 85
Committee of States, 5
communists, KPD
Conservative People's Union, 62
constitution, 1, 2, 5–8, 15, 20, 62
Coolidge, Calvin, 32
Council of Peoples' Commissars (Provisional Government), 3, 4
Cuno, Wilhelm, 23, 27, 31
Curtius, Julius, 95
Czechoslovakia, 12, 27

Danzig, 12
David, Eduard, 75
Dawes Plan, 19, 32–3, 43, 44, 59, 82
Dawes, Charles, 2

DDP (German Democratic Party), 5, 9, 15, 16, 17, 18, 20, 58, 62, 95

Denmark, 12

devaluation, 63

disarmament, 22, 50, 75

Dittmann, Wilhelm, 72, 95

DNVP (Nationalists), 8, 18, 19, 20, 21, 34, 42, 43–4, 55, 61, 64, 66, 69, 82

DVP (German People's Party) 8, 15, 16, 17, 19, 20, 21, 58, 59, 60, 61, 62, 64, 69, 91, 94

East Europe, 11, 13, 27, 28, 34

Ebert, Friedrich, 2, 3, 4, 5, 7, 9, 36, 50, 55, 73, 76, 80, 87, 92

economic developments, 11, 13, 16, 17, 18, 19, 20, 27, 30–5, 39, 58, 59–60, 61, 62–3, 82–84, 95, 96

education, 7, 16, 74, 92

Elbe, 34

employers, 4, 19, 20, 33, 34, 43, 66, 70

Erfurt Programme (1891), 2

Erhardt Brigade, 51

Erzberger, Matthias, 7, 16, 22, 75, 76

Eupen, 12

First World War, 1, 2, 10, 16, 30, 42, 60

Fischer, Ruth, 38

foreign policy, 4, 7, 10–11, 12, 13, 16, 22–8, 52, 79–82

impact of on domestic politics, 9, 13–14, 19–20, 29, 63

foreign trade, 11, 13, 19, 20, 23, 25, 28, 59

Fourteen Points of President Wilson, 10, 12, 75, 76

France, 12, 13, 22, 23, 25, 26, 27, 31, 59, 75, 79, 80, 82, 87, 97

Freikorps, 4, 42, 46, 47, 50, 51, 54, 74, 88

Frick, Wilhelm, 92

'fulfilment', 22, 23, 26, 31, 88

Gauführer, 46

Genoa world economic conference (1922), 24, 25, 31

German Business Party, 21

German Congress of Workers' and Soldiers' Councils, 5

German Empire, 1, 3, 5, 6, 15, 16, 17, 42, 43, 77, 87

German Foreign Office, 10, 23, 81

German minorities, 12, 13, 27, 75

German Revolution, 1–4, 7, 8, 14, 16, 33, 36, 70, 72

Gessler, Otto, 53

Goebbels, Joseph, 98–9

gold standard, 30, 32

Gothein, Georg, 76

Great Britain, 13, 27, 28, 76, 87

'Great Coalition', 7, 18, 58, 61, 97

Groener, General Wilhelm, 3, 53, 56, 62, 68, 93, 94, 97, 98

Haas, August, 96

Haase, Hugo, 2, 3, 72

Hague Conference (1929), 59

Halle Congress, 37

Hammerstein-Equord, General Kurt Freiherr von, 53

Harzburg front, 66, 67

Haussmann, Conrad, 5

Haverstein, Rudolf, 32

Herriot, Edouard, 26

Heye, General Wilhelm, 53, 55

Hilferding, Rudolf, 60, 95

Himmler, Heinrich, 66

Hindenburg, Paul von, 1, 55, 60, 61, 62, 63, 68, 69, 70, 71, 86, 94, 98

Hindenburg, Oscar von, 71

Hitler, Adolf, 5, 14, 42, 43, 44, 55, 64, 66, 67, 69, 70, 71, 85, 86, 87, 90–1

importance in NSDAP, 45, 46, 47, 48, 49, 65

Hoover moratorium (1931), 63
Hörsing, Otto, 54
Hugenberg, Alfred, 43, 44, 59, 61, 62, 71, 85, 86, 97, 98

inflation, 30, 31, 32, 33, 82
Inter-Allied Reparations Commission, 30, 31
'Iron front', 67

Joos, Joseph, 58
judiciary, 7
Junker, 34

Kaas, Monsignor Ludwig, 58, 97
Kaiser Wilhelm II, 1, 2, 22, 51
Kamenev, L. B., 39
KAPD, 37
Kapp, Wolfgang, 37, 43, 51–2, 54, 93
Keynes, Maynard, 11
Kiel, 1
KPD (German Communist Party), 3, 18, 26, 36–41, 47, 48, 59, 62, 69, 84, 85, 86
Kun, Bela, 38
Künstler, Franz, 84–5

Länder, 7, 66
Landsberg, Otto, 73, 76
Latvia, 79
Lausanne conference (1932), 63
League of Nations, 12, 13, 27, 28, 75
Leber, Julius, 56
Lenin, V.I., 23, 38
Levi, Paul, 37, 38
Liebknecht, Karl, 3
Lithuania, 12
Lloyd George, David, 25, 31
Locarno Treaties (1925), 19, 27, 28, 29, 81, 82
London Ultimatum (1921), 22, 31
Ludendorff, General Erich, 1
Luther, Hans, 19, 44
Lüttwitz, General Walther von, 51

Luxemburg, Rosa, 3, 36, 37

Magdeburg Congress (1929), 59
Malmedy, 12
Maltzan, Baron Ago von, 23
'march action'(1921), 38
Marienwerder, 12
Marx, Wilhelm, 19, 44, 58, 8, 82
Maslow, Arkadi, 38
Mecklenburg, 66
Mehring, Franz, 3
Meissner, Otto, 97, 98
Memel, 12
Meyer, Ernst, 38
Moldenhauer, Paul, 60, 61, 95
Moresnet, 12
Moscow, 28, 38, 59
Müller, Hermann, 58, 59, 60, 94, 97
Munich, 46
Munich Soviet (1919), 4

National Assembly, 2, 3, 4, 5, 7, 9, 15, 16, 37, 73
National Liberals, 15, 16
'National Opposition', 59, 63, 66
navy, 50
Neumann, Heinz, 85, 86
New Economic Policy (NEP), 38
North Germany, 36
Noske, Gustav, 4, 51, 52, 54, 73
NSDAP, 1, 36, 44–9, 56, 59, 70, 89–90, 91, 92, 98
   and agriculture, 34, 35, 48, 64, 66, 70
   and Reichswehr, 67–8, 71, 93–4
   clashes with communists, 41, 69
   electoral breakthrough, 61, 62, 64, 65
   party programme, 47–8, 49, 65
Nuremberg, 46

Oberland, 46
Oldenbourg, 66
Organisation Consul, 54
Organisation Escherich, 54

Pan German League, 43, 59, 87
Papen, Franz von, 68, 69, 70, 71
party conflicts, 9, 13, 14, 15, 17,
  18–21, 35, 40, 44, 59, 71, 95, 99
plebiscites, 12
Poincaré, Raymond, 26, 31
Poland, 12, 13, 23, 25, 26, 27, 28,
  29, 38, 79–80
police, 7, 92
Posen, 12
Preuss, Hugo, 5, 6
Prussia, 7, 12, 21, 54, 62, 68, 69,
  86, 93, 94, 99

Radek, Karl, 23
Rapallo, Treaty of (1922), 24, 25,
  26, 28, 31, 80
Rathenau, Walther, 25, 80, 88, 89
rearmament, 23, 37, 63
Red Army, 23
Reich Institute for Unemployment
  Insurance, 59
Reich President, 5–6
Reich Settlement Law, 34
Reichsbahn, 33
Reichsbank, 32, 33
Reichsbanner-Schwartz-Rot-Gold,
  40, 54, 85, 86
Reichslandbund, 43, 65
Reichsrat, 6, 7
Reichstag, 5, 6, 7, 15, 20, 40, 49,
  53, 58, 59, 60, 66, 67, 71, 82,
  95
  elections to, 16, 19, 21, 37, 39, 45,
    61, 62, 64, 68, 69, 78, 85, 99
*Reichsverband der Deutschen
  Industrie*, 65
Reichswehr, 3, 4, 7, 23, 24, 38,
  39, 42, 43, 50–7, 62, 63, 67,
  71, 74, 92–4, 97
Reinhardt, Walther 51
Rentenbank, 32
Rentenmark, 32
reparations, 11, 19, 20, 22, 23, 25,
  30, 31, 31, 33, 59, 60, 63, 75,
  76

Reuter, Ernst, 38
revisionism, 10, 12, 27, 63, 65
Rhineland, 12, 13, 22, 27, 36, 38,
  59, 97
Röhm, Ernst, 47, 66, 68
Rote Frontkämpferbund, 40
Rote Jungfront, 40
Rote Marine, 40
Ruhr crisis (1923), 6, 16, 17, 18,
  23, 26, 31, 32, 42, 56, 82, 83
Russia, *See* Soviet Union
Russian Revolution, 2, 36, 37

SA (*Sturmabteilung*), 46, 47, 64,
  66, 68, 69, 93, 94
Saar, 11, 12
Salomon, Ernst von, 88–9
Salomon, Franz Pfeffer von, 47
Saxony, 36, 38, 39
Schacht, Hjalmar, 65
Scheidemann, Philipp, 9, 10, 73
Schiele, Martin, 61
Schiffer, Eugen, 76
Schleicher, General Kurt von, 53,
  55, 56, 62, 65, 67, 68, 69, 70,
  71, 93, 94, 97, 98
Schleswig, 12, 64, 75
Schroeder, Baron Kurt von, 70
Seeckt, General Hans von, 23, 43,
  52, 53, 54, 55, 56, 79– 80, 92,
  93
self-determination, 12
separatism, 6, 45, 55
Severing, Carl, 86, 93, 94
slump (1929), 17, 49, 58, 60
Soviet Union, 2, 11, 13, 36, 37
  and Germany, 23–6, 28, 38, 39,
    55, 57, 79–80
Spartacists, 3, 4, 36
SPD (German Social Democratic
  Party), 2, 3, 4, 5, 7, 8, 9, 15,
  16, 17, 18, 19, 20, 21, 26, 36,
  38, 40, 48, 52, 56, 58, 59, 60,
  61, 62, 64, 66, 67, 68, 69, 73,
  77, 84–5, 86
SS (*Schutzstaffeln*), 66, 69

'stab in the back' legend, 14, 87
Stahlhelm, 54, 57, 59, 85
Stalin, Joseph, 39, 59
Stegerwald, Adam, 58
Stinnes, Hugo, 16, 34
Strasser, Gregor, 46, 70
Streicher, Julius, 46
Stresemann, Gustav,
  and domestic politics, 16, 17,
    18–19, 31, 55, 59, 94–5
  and foreign policy, 19, 26–9, 44,
    80, 81, 82

taxation, 7, 30, 31, 32, 59, 62–3,
  74
Thälmann, Ernst, 39, 40
Third Reich, 37
Thuringia, 6, 38, 39, 66, 91–2
Thyssen, Fritz, 65
trade unions, 20, 33, 39, 67, 70
Treaty of Riga (1921), 23, 38
Treviranus, Gottfried, 62, 97, 98
Trotsky, Leon, 39
Truppenamt, 57

unemployment, 18, 34, 59, 60, 63,
  65
United States of America, 13, 31,
  32, 33, 76, 87
Upper Silesia, 12
USPD (Independent German Social
  Democratic Party), 2, 3, 4, 36,
  72, 73, 74

Vernunftrepublikaner, 18

Versailles, Treaty of, 1919, 9–14,
  22, 25, 26, 28, 29, 30, 32, 33,
  50, 51, 52, 53, 54, 57, 63,
  75–6, 79, 88, 94
Völkischer Beobachter, 65

Wall Street Crash, 60
'war guilt', 11, 22, 75
Warsaw, 29
'Weimar Coalition', 5, 9, 16, 22,
  62, 66
Weimar Republic, 4, 5, 6, 7, 8, 9,
  13, 15, 18, 30, 33, 34, 44, 70,
  77, 87
  historians on, 1, 14, 21, 35, 36,
    40, 49, 51, 68, 71
  its proclamation, 2, 10
  its downfall, 58
Westarp, Count Cuno, 43, 44
Wiking, 46
Wilson, Woodrow, 10, 12
Wirth, Joseph, 22, 23, 24, 26, 31,
  32, 80, 95
Wissell, Rudolf, 73, 95
Wolff, Theodor, 77, 88
workers, 4, 17, 18, 33, 34, 39, 40,
  48, 76, 84
  and national socialism, 64, 71
Workers' and Soldiers' Councils, 2,
  36, 72

Young Plan, 27, 59, 60, 63, 66,
  97

Zinoviev, Georgy, 37, 39